Edwin H. Atwood

Early history of Maine Pairie, Fair Haven, Lynden, Eden Lake and Paynesville

Edwin H. Atwood

Early history of Maine Pairie, Fair Haven, Lynden, Eden Lake and Paynesville

ISBN/EAN: 9783337714529

Printed in Europe, USA, Canada, Australia, Japan

Cover: Foto ©ninafisch / pixelio.de

More available books at **www.hansebooks.com**

..Early * History..

OF

Maine * Prairie,

FAIR HAVEN, LYNDEN, EDEN LAKE

AND

PAYNESVILLE.

BY

E. H. ATWOOD,

ST. CLOUD, MINN.

History of Maine Prairie.

By E. H. ATWOOD.

FIRST DISCOVERY OF MAINE PRAIRIE.

While gathering statistics and items of interest connected with the stormy times of the Sioux outbreak and massacre of the whites in the summer of 1862, it was suggested that a history of the first discovery and settlement of Maine Prairie would be of value, and the writer was urged to undertake it, beginning with its first discovery by the whites. We often find great differences in the details of scenes and events as related by different individuals, even when they viewed the same occurrences at the same time. The endeavor will be to arrive as nearly as possible at the true account of such historical events as may be deemed worthy of interest.

In the early fifties, there were but few settlements north of St. Paul, and these, with the exception of St. Anthony, were quite small and chiefly confined to the rivers. St. Cloud and Sauk Rapids were the most northern settlements of any size on the Mississippi river. There were a few scattering settlers along the Sauk river; but there was a vast unexplored territory west of the Mississippi and south of the Sauk river, that had probably never been trodden by the foot of the white man. Here was a broad and undefined boundary line between the fierce and warlike tribes of the Sioux Indians on the west and their deadly and bitter foes, the savage tribes of the Chippewas, on the east. The feud between these two tribes had been long, fierce and bloody, and the soil of this region had drank the blood of many of the braves of both Sioux and Chippewas. In this region there was plenty of game. The wild deer roamed almost unmolested. The otter, mink, muskrat, and other fur bearing animals, were found in great numbers around the thousands of lakes. Wolves, wild cats, lynx and coyotes were found roaming unmolested, for the hunter from either tribe well knew the perils that awaited him should he venture upon this disputed territory. Should any hunter not return from an expedition in this direction his tribe well knew that his scalp was dangling at the belt of some warrior of the hostile tribe. If this happened, fierce war was made to avenge the loss, and in the sanguinary conflict that followed many brave warriors of both tribes lost their lives. These conflicts continued at intervals for some time after the territory was occupied by the white settlers, the last one in this section occuring in the spring of 1860, in the town of Maine Prairie.

Such were the conditions of this territory, when, in the year 1854, a number of families living in the state of Massachusetts decided to emigrate in a body and form a settlement by themselves in some new western state.

These people were intelligent, and liberal in their views, and wished to form a settlement with people of broad and progressive minds, so that their churches and schools might be conducted in accordance with their advanced standard of truth and progress. The agents whom they sent out to find a suitable location for their settlement came up the Mississippi to Clearwater, in the fall of 1854, and started westward into this unknown region. James Campbell, brother of the late Mrs. J. E. West, accompained these agents from Clearwater.

VIEWING THE PROMISED LAND.

A slight snow storm somewhat bewildered them, but they soon came upon what is now known as Maine Prairie. As they stood upon a commanding hill and gazed upon the beautiful plain spread out before them, dotted with many beautiful groves, with innumerable lakes flashing in the bright sunlight, surrounded on all sides with a dense growth of timber, they were enraptured with the glorious scene. Coming as they had from the rugged and mountainous regions of Massachusetts, they were unused to such a landscape. They stood entranced with the grand and beautiful picture of green plains, beautiful groves and glistening lakes. With hushed and baited breath, they drank in the glorious panorama, and enthusiastically exclaimed: "Here is what we have been looking for! Here is where we will found our grand colony." The inspiration of such a glorious country cannot fail to inspire the hearts of our children with a higher and nobler idea of life. Here we can surround them with all that will make them better men and women!" They christened the place "Paradise." After some further explorations, they undertook to again find their "Paradise," but after repeated efforts, they were unable to do so, and those that were to form the colony, thus became somewhat scattered, and settled in different parts of the state. The golden dreams that they had cherished of a colony of intelligent, progressive and advanced thinkers, where they could rear their children in the atmosphere of the highest ideal attainment of human life, were unrealized. When the agents could not find their "Paradise," they then called it "Paradise Lost."

Whether the world has lost or gained by their failure to establish a colony or not, is hard to tell. It may be that the good influence which each member of this community exerted in different localities has proved a stronger force for good than they could have exerted if they had united in one isolated colony.

SECOND DISCOVERY AND SETTLEMENT IN 1856.

From the fall of 1854 until the spring of 1856, nothing definite had been learned of Maine Prairie. In February of that year A. B. and A. S. Greely and A. Messer, who had come out from Maine the fall before, and had remained at St. Anthony during the winter, heard of Maine Prairie from Mr. Henry Johnson, who kept a hotel at Neenah, six miles south of St. Cloud. They came up on foot, but did not quite reach the Prairie, and returned to St. Anthony. On the 10th of March A. B. Greely and wife, A. S. Greely, A. Messer and Ansel Crommnett left St. Anthony for Maine Prairie. In due time they reached Little Prairie, three miles west of Neenah and five miles from Maine Prairie. Here they built a built a log house and began house keeping. Mrs. A. B. Greely was the first white woman that had penetrated thus far. Mr. H. Dam and a few others joined them here. After their house was built, the men began to search for the "lost Paradize." It is claimed that Mr. Messer was the first to discover the Prairie, and staked out the first claim for himself, and one for Albert Staples, in the northeast corner of the Prairie, H. Dam taking an adjoining claim. April 10th, A. B. and Horace Greely staked out claims for themselves near Carnelian Lake, and commenced a claim shanty.

A few days later, A. S. Greely and Ansel Crommett, in looking over the Prairie for a good location, ascended a high bluff south of the Prairie. The view from this place was grand, and filled the heart of the prospectors with delight. They counted thirteen lakes that lay beneath them, sparkling in the morning sun. One lake in particular attracted their attention. It was a beautiful sheet of water and lay like a pearl set in emerald. It was afterwards named Pearl Lake. Adjoining it, they saw what they had been looking for: Wood, and water and prairie. They started for the lake in haste, fearing others might appropriate their prize, paced off, staked and marked their claims, but in their excitement their strides were too long, and their claims contained enough for four settlers. This land they held and shared with their brothers, N T. Greely and J. O. Crommett, when they arrived the next fall.

About the 1st of May, A. B. and A. S. Greely, H. Dam, Dudley French, A. Messer and J. H French cut out a road through the timber from their home on Little Prairie to Maine Prairie. A. S. Greely's ox team accompained them, being the first team through. Mrs H Dam soon came through with her husband, being the first white women to arrive on Maine Prairie. Soon after the road was cut through, many other settlers from the east began to arrive.

MANY SETTLERS ARRIVE.

The fame of the beautiful Prairie, with its sparkling lakes, its rich soil, and beautiful groves, had reached back to Maine, and other Eastern States, and during the spring and summer of 1856 the following people arrived and took up claims: D. W. Fowler, F. H. Dam, Joseph Dam, Joseph and Samuel Young, Wm. Heywood, J. H. French, Albert Staples, Wm. Milligan, Horace Greely, M. Greely, Hiram Millett, Moses Ireland, John Farwell, O Farwell, F. M. Kimball, R. F. Adley, James Taylor, Geo. Clark, Daniel Spaulding, Ruel Furlong, Miss Marilla and Almira French, John Guptil, James Simmons, D. Sutherland, D. A. Hoyt, S. Leavett, Aaron Scribner, Andrew F. and Daniel Perkins, Wm.

Stewart, Henry Hutchinson and Doc. Mayo. All of these took claims during the spring and summer of 1856. Most of these early settlers were from the state of Maine, which will probably explain, why they named their town Maine Prairie.

Moses Ireland laid out and plated the town-site on the west shore of Carnelian Lake, September 7th, 1856, and called it Marysville. The location was beautiful, and undoubtedly the proprietor expected to soon see a thriving and prosperous city flourishing upon his town-site. But, like many others in the new state, it never rose above a paper town-site.

GRASSHOPPER VISITATION OF 1856.

In the fall of 1856 swarms of grasshoppers, or locusts, alighted on some of the farms, and deposited their eggs. The next spring the young ones damaged M. Greely's crops, and about the middle of July an immense swarm alighted on his farm, covering the ground and eating up all that the others had left. They all left the same day, leaving the few fields, denuded of all crops.

MINISTERS AND CHURCHES

Alvin Messer, a Baptist Minister, preached in the town in 1856, the services being held in private residences, he soon left, and Rev. Inman, a Close Communion Baptist took his place. In the early sixties, the frame of a Baptist church building was erected, but on account of the war, never was finished. In 1879 the present church was built and dedicated.

In 1857, Rev. Levi Gleason was sent by the Methodists to Maine Prairie, and held occasional services in private residences and school houses. In 1873, the present church was built, being the first church building in the town. The Methodist was the strongest church for many years.

GROWTH OF THE COLONY.

The winter of 1856-57 passed quietly. The pioneers worked hard making their houses and stables comfortable. The next summer a few more home-seekers arrived and took land. In June, T. B. Stanley came from Trumball County, Ohio, and took up a claim in section 2, and in 1858 erected a house and barn. In 1859, he brought out his wife and four sons, D. B., Joseph, Plum and Roger. In 1857, among others who arrived were A. Manervey and family, Thomas Cadwell and wife, Geo. W. Cutter and family, D. A. Roberts and wife, Alex. Spaulding and wife, Thomas Steen and wife, Elder T. E. Inman and wife, Willard Spanlding, S. F. Brown, wife and son, S. F., O. S. Senter, John Guptil's wife and family, and John White.

INDIANS.

During the winter, numerous bands of of Indians camped in the neighborhood for short periods, for the purpose of hunting. They were generally peaceably inclined, and frequently visited the settlers' houses. They often visited the house of M. Greely. Mr. Greely worked in the woods that winter, leaving home in the morning and returning at night. But Mrs. Greely was not afraid of the Indians, and often gave them food, or let them warm themselves by the fire. One day, an Indian came in who had often been there before. He made a great many demands until Mrs. Greely becoming tired, told him to "Go!" when he made an insulting remark. Seizing a pitchfork and pointing it at his eyes, she again said go! He looked at her a moment and departed. In a few days, he came again. Mrs. Greely did not wait for him to say anything but reaching up to the beams overhead took down Mr. Greely's sword and again said to Mr. Chippewa, "Git!" He went out very sullenly, and seeing a fine large steer standing near, drove him into the deep snow so that only his head was visible. He remained in that predicament until the next day, when Mr. G. found him. After this, Mrs. Greely could always tell the near presence of Indians by the intense fright of that steer.

FIRST FOURTH OF JULY CELEBRATION.

On July 4, 1857, the pioneers celebrated the nation's natal day by a public picnic in the O. Farwell grove, on the shore of Carnelian Lake. Elder T. E.

Inman delivered the oration. This was the first time that the glorious Fourth of July had been celebrated in this vast region.

AS FIRST ORGANIZED.

The town of Maine Prairie, as first organized, consisted of what is now the towns of Rockville, Fair Haven and Maine Prairie, and was organized in accordance with and pursuant to an order of the Board of County Commissioners of the county of Stearns, issued on the 20th day of May, 1858. The following is the—

NOTICE!

Notice is hereby given, that on the 27th day of May, A. D. 1858, an election will be held at the house of John Farwell, in and for the town of Marysville, Stearns Co unty, Minnesota, for the purpose of electing the following town officers, to-wit: 3 Supervisors, one of whom shall be designated as Chairman; 1 Town Clerk, 1 Assessor, 1 Collector, 1 Overseer of the Poor, 2 Constables, 2 Justices of the Peace, and as many overseers of roads as Road Districts.

Per order of the Board of County Commissioners.

"Dated, Saint Cloud, May 20, 1858.
JOSEPH EDELBROCK.
"A true copy, attest:
"M. GREELY, Town Clerk."

MINUTES OF MEETING.

"According to the foregoing notice, the voters of the town mentioned met at the place designated, occupied John Farwell's log granery, and proceeded as follows:

"The meeting was called to order by John Farwell, and on motion Orlen Farwell was chosen moderator, and M. Greely clerk.

"On motion of M. Greely, it was voted that the name of the town be Maine Prairie.

"Then proceeded to ballot for town officers, with the following result: For supervisors, G. W. Cutter, chairman; Daniel Spaulding, Thos. Partridge; town clerk, M. Greely; assessor, A. H. Staples, J K. Noyes and I. N. Berlin assistant assessors; constables, A. B. Greely and W. H. Day; Justices of the peace, O. Farwell and A. B. Gaylord; collector, H. P. Bennett; overseer of the poor, O. S. Senter.

"Voted that the next meeting be held at D. Spaulding's."
"Attest: O. FARWELL, Moderator.
M. GREELY, Clerk.
"A true copy: Attest, M. Greely."

FURTHER ORGANIZATION.

As many of the officers of the new town elected at the town meeting neglected to qualify, the following petition was presented to M. Greely, town clerk:

"To Martin Greely, Esq., clerk of the town of Maine Prairie: The undersigned would respectfully petition that a meeting of the legal voters of said town be called as soon as may be, at the most central point, for the purpose of setting off road districts, choosing and qualifying town officers; and as in duty bound will ever pray."

"Maine Prairie, July 29, 1859, A. H. Staples, O. S. True, J. H. French, H. P. Bennett, John P. Guptill, Sumner Leavett, H. Dam, D. S. French, A. S. Greely, D. Spaulding, A. Spaulding, Geo. W. Cutter, Jesse Lee Smith."

A town meeting was held in compliance with the petition and the vacant offices filled. The town was divided into six road districts.

THE USUAL TOWN HALL.

On the 23rd of October, 1858, a meeting of the legal voters was called and it was voted to erect a town house and to raise the sum of $500 to build it.

Daniel Spaulding, R. F. Adley and John Farwell were chosen a committee to build it. "H. Dam, M. Greely and John Farwell were chosen a committee to locate the house, their decision to be final. The town house seems to have "died abornin," as no further mention is made of it.

A PIONEER PIC-NIC.

S. F. Brown and wife and Martin Greely and wife, celebrated the 4th of July, 1858, in truly pioneer if not patriotic style. As provisions were scarce, it taxed the ingenuity of the women to find dainties enough for the pic-nic dinner. The common bill of fare for every day consisted of pork, bread and molasses, but that was not sufficently elaborate for this occasion. Mrs. Greely went into the fields and picked enough of wild oxalis (or sorrei) to make a pie. This sorrel somewhat resembles rhubarb in taste. Mrs. Brown contributed a fruit cake, which she had brought from her old home in Massachusetts the fall before. They remember this dinner with a great deal of pleasure.

DOINGS IN 1858.

Among the arrivals this year (1858) were Joseph Eaton, wife and children, and Mr. Scheelar.

In February, 1858, as related by James Kimball, as a party of ten or twelve Chippewas were passing Mr. Thos. Straw's place, they broke into his shanty and stole all the flour he had. Mr. Straw arrived home with his ox team shortly after they had left. The loss of his provision filled him with anger, and leaving his team, he bravely started with his goad stick on the trail of the robbers. He soon caught up with them and began belaboring the nearest Indian with his gad, the others looking on and laughing at their unfortunate brother, but soon they all pulled the ramrods from their guns and began to retaliate, causing Straw to beat a hasty retreat, somewhat the worse for the conflict

In the fall of 1858, a band of Sioux were camped near Willow Creek, on the prairie, on a hunting expedition. While thus occupied one of their tribe was accidently shot and killed. As he was being brought to camp by his comrades the mourners met them wailing their mournful death dirge and wringing their hands and filling the air with their wild death songs. The next morning their camp was found deserted, whether through superstitious fears or from some other cause, is not known.

INCIDENTS.

From 1858 to 1862 wheat was worth about 35 cents per bushel, in store pay. Once in a while Proctor & Clark could be induced to pay a little money. The prevailing costum for the men during this time was made from grain sacks. A. S. Greely had marked a lot of new sacks by pressing them against the greasy cogs of the bull wheel of his horse power, which left an imprint very unique and not easily counterfeited. It consisted of three black

marks two inches long. The story goes
that this peculiar mark was found upon
the newly made pants of people who had
barrowed sacks of Greely, unbeknown to
that gentleman. A. S. Greely ran the
first reaper, and in connection with A. B.
Greely, operated the first threshing
machine and took their pay in grain, taking every ninth bushel.

The following appeared in the St. Cloud
Democrat of Aug. 12, 1858:

"A Maine Prairieite says: 'We have
crops enough on Maine Prairie to supply
all northern Minnesota,' and a Rockville-
ite says: 'You ought to see the crops up
the Sauk towards Rockville, I don't know
what they are going to do with them."

From the St. Cloud *Democrat*, May 20,
1858: "The country around St. Cloud,
west of the Mississippi was purchased of
the Indians in a treaty made with them
by Hon. Alexander Ramsey and Luke
Lee, in 1852, and ratified by the senate the
same year. The Sioux had owned this
land from 1827 but had not occupied it,
and it was used as a hunting ground by
Winnebagoes, whose land reached within
four miles north of St. Cloud."

The following extract is taken from the
St. Cloud *Democrat*, Dec. 9th, 1858: "Rev.
T. E. Inman, of the Baptist church, has
killed eight deer this season. Mr. Inman
is a regular pioneer preacher of the John
the Baptist class, who eat locust and wild
honey, and are clothed in camel's hair,
and have leather girdles about their loins.
He spends his Sabbaths and part of other
days preaching the Gospel in destitute
places, and in a great measure supports
his family by his rifle."

POST OFFICE AND MAILS.

A Post Office was established in the Farwell grove and called after the town-site
Marysville. Orlan Farwell was appointed
the first Post Master. The mail was received once a week. After a number of
years a tri-weekly mail was obtained and
in 1861 Alex. Spaulding was appointed
Post Master. The office was established
at the "Corners," and the name changed
to Maine Prairie. In a few years a daily
mail arrived, and in 1867 the present Post
Master, D. B. Stanley, was appointed, and
has held the office ever since, except two
years.

Hattie, daughter of Dudley French was
the first child born in the town. Joseph
Mitchell and Sarah Greely were the first
to marry in the town, in 1858.

SECOND TOWN MEETING, 1859.

The second annual town meeting was
held April 5th, 1859, at the store house of
G. W. Cutter, on the west side of Pearl
lake. This was a meeting long to be remembered. The old settlers refer to it
with the remark that "they had a high
old time," and the animosities engendered
at that meeting, although dormant, could
easily be aroused 35 years afterwards by
making inquiries about the meeting, when
there were those present who had been
opponents in the conflict. The victorious
party elected M Hanson, Chairman, and
P. Mouse and Wm. Shaffer, supervisors;
and M. Greely, Clerk. Many roads were
laid out this year.

April 5th, of this year the township of
Fair Haven was detached and organized
into a separate town.

"THE SCHOOL MA'AM'S ROAD."

In the summer of 1859, Miss Anna
Maria Boobar, of Fair Haven, taught a
school in Horace Greely's house. She
boarded at Mr. Leavitt's and had to walk
to and from her school through the tall
wet grass. Soon some of the gallant young
men took a breaking plow and made a
good road, by plowing the grass under.
This ridge ran diagonally across the
prairie, and remained for many years,
occasioning a great deal of curiosity and
many inquiries on the part of new comers
and strangers, for the Horace Greely
house was soon moved away and the
"School Ma'am's road," as it was called,
seemed to start at no particular point and
to end in the same manner.

ABOUT EARLY SCHOOLS.

Among the new settlers who arrived in
1859 were B. H. Winslow and family,

Charles Neal and Isaac Bently, with his mother and sister Julia.

A school house was built near where the Baptist church now stands, and during that winter logs were hauled for the school house in district No. 28. The house was erected the next spring, on the west shore of Pearl lake, M. Greely was elected director, S. F. Brown, clerk, and A. Maservey, treasurer. The first school in this district was taught in the summer of 1860, by Miss Carrie Hicks, (now Mrs. Wm. L Heywood.) Miss Lizzie Rice, of Fair Haven, taught this school in 1861, and Miss Philena Fields taught it in 1862.

The Stanley school house in district No. 29, called the "Red School House," was built in 1860. T. B. Stanley and Dudley French were the first officers. The first school in this district was taught by Miss Dean, of Fair Haven, and Miss Julia Hicks taught the next school in the summer of 1861. In district No. 30 Mrs. Alonzo Spaulding taught the spring term in Daniel Spaulding's log house, and Miss Carrie Hicks taught the fall term in the same house in 1860. The school house in this district was built in 1861. The first officers were John Farwell, R. F. Adley and F. M. Kimball. It is generally known as the Farwell school house.

INDIANS CAUSE UNEASINESS.

While the settlers were busy with their labors in the fall of 1859, there was much uneasiness among them on account of the encampment, in the southern part of the town, of bands of Sioux indians. The citizens of Cold Spring had also become alarmed on account of the numerous bands of Sioux hunters roaming through the country, and had sent to St. Cloud for a company of men to go to Cold Springs and assist the citizens in driving away a band that had become very troublesome. Although these indians were at peace with the whites, still there existed a feeling among them that the land was theirs, and that they had been defrauded of their just rights.

AN INDIAN FIGHT.

There were rumors that there had been several encounters between marauding bands of Sioux and Chippewas in the towns of Maine Prairie and Fair Haven, and in the timber to the south, with more or less fatal results. The feeling of fear and distrust among the white settlers was greatly intensified by a tragic event that occurred soon after. At the time the Sioux were encamped upon the prairie, two young and brave Chippewas were trapping upon the waters to the south of the Pra rie. The Sioux were not long in discovering the signs of their deadly foes, but were unable to capture them. Later they succeeded in discovering and plundering the camp of the Chippewas, and destroying their entire outfit. This so enraged the young braves that they decided that nothing but the scalp of a Sioux brave would average their loss and retrieve their wounded honor. With a desire for revenge burning in their hearts, they boldly sought a spot near the hostile camp. Secreeting themselves, they awaited the return of the Sioux hunters to their camp after a day's chase. The boldness of this move on the part of the Chippewas was unparalleled in the annals of Indian warfare. Here were two Indians within half a mile of fifty or a hundred fierce Sioux warriors, and knowing that at the sound of the first gun they would bring the whole encampment after them. Still their fierce desire for revenge caused take them to the terrible risk. They had not long to wait, a party of Sioux hunters passed near them. The battle which followed was quick, fierce and bloody, one Sioux was killed and others wounded. They returned the fire killing one Chippewa and severely wounded the other, but, though badly wounded, the surviving Chippewa sprang upon his deadly foe, tore the bloody scalp from his head while he was still struggling in the last throes of death, then with a wild exultant war whoop, which was heard throughout the hostile camp he dashed through the bush and timber and plunged into a lake. In an incredible short time the shore was lined with Sioux warriors who tried to gain the opposite shore in time to intercept him as he emerged from the water, but he succeeded in gaining a safe hiding place upon the opposite shore, where he lay concealed for several days. He then made his way to the house of James Simmons, with whom he was acquainted, who secreted him in his cellar, and, although the Sioux were searching for him, and came to the house several times, failed in their search. Simmons succeeded, after several days, in covering him up in a wagon and taking him off in safety, with the Sioux scalp dangling at his belt. The body of the dead Chippewa was placed upon a pile of dry brush and surrounded by a circle of Sioux, who emptied their guns into it. The pile was then set on fire while the Sioux leaped and shouted around the burning mass until all was consumed. This scene was witnessed by D. A. Roberts, and never, as long as life lasts, will the impression of this wild scene be effaced from his memory.

PRESENT TOWN ORGANIZED, 1860.

The third annual town meeting was held at the house of G. Bauer, April 3d, 1860. The Rockville people captured about all the town offices.

The citizens of Maine Prairie organized the present town, pursuant to the following "notice:"

"St. Cloud, June 5, 1860.

"Daniel Spaulding and others greeting:

Your township, and the fraction of (21) (I think) was this day set off by the county board into a separate town, to be called Maine Prairie, and your town meeting is to be held at the house of Daniel Spaulding, on Monday, the 25th instant.

"STEPHEN MILLER."

"A true copy. Attest: S. F. Brown, Town Clerk."

The following officers were chosen at this first town meeting of Maine Prairie proper: Supervisors, T. B. Stanley, chairman, J Eaton, D. Spaulding; town clerk, S. F. Brown; treasurer, R. F. Adley; justice of the peace, Orlen Farwell; superintendent of schools, S. F. Brown; constables, Wm. Milligan and F. M. Kimball; overseer of the poor, A. B. Groely.

Rockville was organized into a separate town, June 25th, 1860, and Maine Prairie was left with one and one-half townships.

THE FOUNDER OF YARMOUTH.

Geo. W. Cutter was quite a prominent figure in the affairs of town and county. In 1858, he had surveyed and platted the town of "Yarmouth," on the west side of Pearl Lake, built a house and large barn and store. He placed the lots in the town of Yarmouth on the market, and regretted his inability to go East and sell them at fabulous prices. He was county commissioner.

In May, of 1860, he left with his family for the east, and the bright anticipations of seeing the town of Yarmouth develop into a mighty city vanished with him. His old haunts saw him no more.

THE USUAL "INDIAN SCARE."

On the 8th of July, 1860, a wild rumor came to the Prairie that a vast horde of savage Sioux Indians were on the warpath and were sweeping down from the west, murdering and torturing the inhabitants and burning their buildings, leaving a blackened trail of death and desolation in their wake. A panic seized the citizens. All the women and children were hastily started for St. Cloud, accompanied by some of the older men. In their fright they took only those things that were handiest and would be most needed, and poured into St. Cloud. Some traveled with horse teams, some with oxen, and some on foot. The citizens of St. Cloud opened wide their doors, and took the panic-stricken refugees in, and kindly cared for them. It was rumored that the last ones that left the Prairie could see the flames of the burning buildings, and hear the shrieks of the victims as they were being tortured by the savages. A large number of the men remained on the Prairie, and met at the house of Daniel Spaulding, where they were drilled by Capt. Inman, and all possible preparation made to resist the Indians.

They bravely determined to stay and fight for their homes and not leave unless overpowered by superior numbers. There was an independent company of militia at St. Cloud, with Mr. C. Lueg as captain. When the rumor of the advance of the savages (estimated at twenty thousand) reached St. Cloud, the members of this company were hastily assembled, with what arms and ammunition they could collect, and bravely rode out to meet the advancing hosts. The remaining citizens cleaned up their old guns, collected ammunition and made preparations to give the savages a warm reception should they reach the town. In St. Cloud, a large number of the men remained up all that night to watch. All were anxious to learn the fate of the men who had gone forward to meet the Indians. About three o'clock the next morning a half-breed on the east side, wishing to come across the river, gave a prolonged whoop to awaken the ferry man. As the blood curdling sound rang out on the still night air and reached the ears of anxious watchers, it was thought by some of them that it was a veritable war whoop, and that the Indians were about to attack the place.

The little band of pioneers of Maine Prairie were greatly relieved when they saw the company of soldiers from Saint Cloud coming to assist them. They could get no reliable information as to the movements of the Indians. Thomas Straw volunteered to go forward and reconnoiter and obtain information regarding the locality and numbers of the invading horde. He boldly started that night and reached Forest City, without discovering any Indians. He there ascertained that the whole thing was a false alarm, and that there were no Indians within a long distance. Early the next morning the soldiers returned to St. Cloud, and the people returned to their homes.

During the summer of this year, 1860, E. H. Atwood purchased the farm of Ansel Crommet, situated on the south shore of Pearl Lake, built a house and moved into it in the fall. He came from Illinois, accompanied by his wife and son, Clarence L.

Wm. H. Day settled in the town this year.

The St. Cloud *Democrat* of Feb. 10, 1860, has the following: "A donation party was given at the house of Deacon Dam, to Elder Inman. A very delightful affair. Parties from St. Cloud and Fair Haven assisted in the success of the affair."

A. S. Greely and Miss Eliza Clark were married Friday, June 15th, 1860.

CHIPPEWA-SIOUX BATTLE OF 1860.

The different accounts given the writer of the battle between the Sioux and Chippewas on Maine Prairie, on Saturday, May 12, 1860, by different citizens who lived on the Prairie at that time, are somewhat conflicting. There was a wide difference between the numbers said to be engaged, and the number killed and wounded. But it is believed that the account given below is substantially correct.

A party of ten young Sioux warriors and one Winnebago started out from their reservation on the warpath for Chippewa scalps. On their way up to Crow Wing, where they expected to surprise and capture Chippewas, they crossed Maine Prairie, and stopped at Orlan Farwell's to obtain something to eat. They informed him that they were going after Chippewa scalps. As some of their guns were out of order, they got H. P. Bennett to repair them. They went up and scouted around the Chippewa settlement, near Crow Wing. They surprised and came near capturing a young squaw, but she escaped by diving into the Mississippi river, and swimming to the opposite shore. After this they found the grave of the father of Hole-in-the-day and dug up and burned the bones. Hole-in-the-day was a celebrated Chippewa chief, living at Crow Wing. He had a number of wives, one being a white woman. On one of his visits to Washington he had been presented with a fine Colt's revolving rifle. The Sioux finding that they could get no scalps started back, reaching St. Cloud the next morning, on the East side of the river. Philip Beaupre was running the ferry and the Sioux tried to get him to ferry them over, but, knowing that they had been after scalps, he refused to do so. He also soon discovered that Hole-in-the-day with a band of braves, was secreeted on the west side of the river watching every movement of their foes. The Chippewa chief had learned of the desecration of his father's grave, and hastily gathering a few warriors he swiftly descended on the west side of the river, hoping to ambush the Sioux as they crossed the river, failing in this they watched them all day,

Hole-in-the-day, with whom Mr. Beaupre was acquainted, urged him to ferry the Sioux over, so they could have a good chance to ambush them, as they landed, but Mr. Beaupre very wisely declined to assist either party. That night the Sioux succeeded in crossing the river, and started for their reservation. They had no idea that they were being pursued and when they arrived at Maine Prairie, they felt quit safe and went to different houses to get something to eat. They stole a lot of eggs and a pair of shoes from O. Farwell. While thus engaged Hole-in-the-day and his band, who had taken their trail early in the morning, had passed around the prairie and secreted themselves in a patch of hazel brush to the south of where the present Farwell school house stands, and near the trail by which the Sioux would pass when they started to return. It was not long before they saw their enemies advancing along the trail single file all unconsious of the fate awaiting them.

Each Chippewa selected his victim and all fired simultaneously. With a fearful yell five of their number leaped high in

the air and fell mortally wounded. Some of them seeing no escape, cut their own throats rather than suffer torture at the hands of their merciless enemies. Hole-in-the-Day now handled his Colt's revolving rifle with fearful effect. Five were killed and left on the field, two were very badly wounded but they succeeded in getting into the brush and escaped capture. Four got away, but three of them were wounded and only one escaped unhurt. Hole-in the-Day was the only Chippewa wounded, and he only slightly. The dead Sioux were scalped and the Winnebago's head was cut off. The bodies of the slain were greatly disfigured. The head and the scalps were exhibited with boisterous demonstrations of joy to a number of the white settlers. Hole-in-the-Day had eight warriors with him in the fight. After several days, the whites buried the dead Indians. Seven days later, seventy-five Sioux warriors and several squaws came and dug up the dead, washed them and wrapped them in new blankets and reburied them. One of those that had crawled into the brush was found dead. The other was still alive, having lain seven days without attendance or anything to eat or drink. The dead one and the wounded one were taken back by the Sioux. It is said that the scalped ones are always buried where they fall, and never taken back to their home. A scalped Indian seems to be in disgrace.

The stolen shoes were found on a dead Indian with a bullet hole through one of them. The head of the Winnebago was presented to a St. Cloud physician by Hole-in-the-Day.

After the fight the Chippewas came to the house of Daniel Spaulding, and feeling greatly elated over their victory they emptied the head and scalps out on the floor at the same time yelling and boasting that they were "Big Indians." Mrs. Spaulding was alone, and was badly frightened at sight of the bloody trophies, and the wild whoops of the savages.

THE WAR BETWEEN THE STATES

During the summer of 1861, there was much excitement occasioned by the southern rebellion. A volunteer company was organized and frequently drilled. Meetings were held and patriotic speeches were made. On the 4th of July the company was drilled. They made a splendid appearance, and many offered to enlist for the war. Captain T. E. Inman made a thrilling speech, which aroused the patriotism of the people to the highest pitch. The crops were gathered in and preparations were made by many to enlist, should the war continue. It was the hope of all that the war would soon end, and their services would not be needed.

President Lincoln's call for more troops banished all hopes of a speedy termination of the conflict. The Minnesota 4th Regiment was being formed, and Captain Inman offered his services and was enrolled Oct. 10th, 1861, and mustered in as Captain of Company D. The following are the names of Maine Prairieites that were enrolled in his company: I. N. Bently, Geo. A. Clark, Thomas Cadwell, Edward J. French, Quartus Farwell, Horace S. Greely, Albert Guptill, John P. Guptill, D. J. Hanscom Ezra G. Hicks, Edwin Kidder, W. A. Milligan, Charles Neal, Daniel F. Perkins, William H. Stewart, J. C. Winslow, Albana Wade, S. F. Brown, Aaron Scribner and Thos. Straw.

Andrew F. Perkins enlisted in Nov., 1861, in the 1st Minnesota Regiment. David Spaulding, Alonzo Spaulding, John Widert, John Greely, David Goodner, Alberton Whitney and Thomas Falone, enlisted in different regiments, the three last in 1865, and went south; while W. W. Clark, Chester Clark and Albert Guptill enlisted in the 2nd Minnnesota Cavalry, and were sent out to scout on the western frontier. Thomas O. and George Spaulding enlisted with Capt. Oscar Taylor, and fought Indians on the plains. This makes thirty-two that volunteered from our town. Of the above volunteers, four never returned. Horace Greely died at St. Anthony, Minn., on his way home in 1863; John P. Guptill died April 24, 1863, in a floating hospital at Nashville; Daniel F. Perkins was killed May 22, 1863, in battle at Vicksburg; Alberton Whitney died in 1865. The few men left at home had to work hard to take care of their farms for there were no men that could be hired.

PRIVATIONS OF EARLY PIONEERS.

Nothing has been said so far of the suffering and privations of the early pioneers. The means of nearly all of them had been exhausted by the expense incurred in moving out to this country, and in improvements; in purchasing provisions and seeds. They expected to raise enough the first summer for their own food, but the locusts came and devoured most of their crops. The winter of 1856 7 was a hard one for the settlers. Provisions had to be hauled from St. Anthony. The closest economy had to be used in keeping down expenses, and such luxuries as tea, sugar and coffee were seldom used. In the spring of 1857, great difficulty was experienced in procuring seed to plant their fields. But they were finally seeded, and there was a good prospect of an abundant crop, when, just before the time for harvest to begin, an immense swarm of locusts alighted and in one day these ravenous pests devoured their entire crop.

The winter of 1857-8 will long be remembered by those early pioneers. With their crops destroyed, their funds exhausted and much of their property mortgaged, and a long cold winter before them, the prospects were gloomy enough to appall the stoutest heart. But these people were not easily discouraged. They had to economize in every possible way. Fish and wild game of all kinds were made use of for food to help out their slender store of provisions. Some of the families at times had but one or two articles of food in the house. For shoes and clothing the strictest economy had to be practiced. Old boot tops were taken by the women and made into shoes for the children, often using heavy cloth or felt for all but the soles, and sometimes a man would take the boot tops of last winter's wear and make a pair of moccasins for the next winter's use. After his woolen pants had been very much demoralized and unpresentable in polite society, and his coat and vest would let the gentle zephers of summer or the fierce blizzards perambulate unchecked around his body, he would, by some method wholly unexplainable, procure some heavy white ducking, and his wife would make a pair of overalls and a "warmus," the one to cover his pants and the other to hide the defects of his coat. Then for a few weeks, while this new over suit was clean and his head covered with a coon skin cap of home manufacture, he felt in a condition to attend church. During all of this time the hearts of the settlers never failed them. They were cheerful and hopeful. Their morning cup of coffee, made of roasted peas or dried bread crusts browned, often without sweetening, was relished by those whose appetites were stimulated by healthy exercise. With unflinching courage they procured seed to sow their lands in the spring of 1858. The good soil of Minnesota responded nobly and their crops were good, but it took several years to recover from their loss and pay old debts and begin to live.

THE SIOUX OUTBREAK OF 1862.

During the outbreak of the Sioux Indians, in the summer of 1862, there were many acts of bravery, many deeds of valor, many scenes of heroic unselfish devotion of man to man, and many exciting incidents that the historian has never chronicled, and which are only remembered by the few survivors who are first passing to that bourne from whence none returneth. Although the numbers engaged in deadly conflict with their relentless and savage foes were small and insignificant, in comparison to the vast armies that were engaged in putting down the rebellion, yet in true bravery, heroism and courage, these pioneers were unsurpassed by any of their brethren on southern battle fields. The future history of Minnesota, and especially of the events occurring during the progress of the massacre of the whites in 1862, by the Sioux Indians, would be incomplete without an account of the thrilling events that transpired in the many isolated little hamlets and settlements upon the extreme frontier of the young state. None of the historians of that eventful period have mentioned the prominent part taken by the people of Maine Prairie in the brave stand they made for their homes. And, as the principal actors of those stormy days are fast passing away, it was deemed advisable to record as many of the leading events of that period, participated in by the people of that isolated settlement as could be found.

THE GREAT SIOUX OUTBREAK.

The town of Maine Prairie is situated fifteen miles southwest of St. Cloud. The prairie proper is irregular in shape, from four to five miles across, and, in 1862, had about fifty-five American families, with a few German families in the northwest corner. It the fall of 1861, Capt. Inman had organized company D. 4th regiment, for the war, in which about 22 had enlisted from our town. Besides these several others had enlisted in other regiments. After doing duty at Fort Abercrombie during the winter, they started the next April for the seat of war, leaving about thirty-five men, not including a number of quite old men, and a few boys, in the town. There were but two or three reapers on the prairie, the grain being bound on the ground by hand, and needing from six to nine men to make a full crew. The harvest that year was very heavy and late. It was impossible to hire men to help harvest, and the only way for a farmer to get his grain cut was to join a crew and follow a reaping machine. In this way he helped others and they in turn were to assist him. We had been harvesting but a few days, when, about the 19th of August, a rumor was brought that the Sioux Indians, near Yellow Medicine, had killed some of the whites. It was thought to be only a

drunken row, and no alarm was felt. A
heavy rain falling that afternoon
stopped the reaping for the next day, and
a number of the settlers on horseback
happened to meet near the center of the
Prairie. Among the number were A. B.
Greely, E. H. Atwood, D. A. Hoyt and
A. S. Greely. Rumors of more Indian
depredations had been heard, and some
alarm was felt. After discussing the subject a while, it was voted that E. H. Atwood and A. B. Greely should go to
Fair Haven, and further, if necessary,
to obtain some definite information regarding the truth of the rumors. If there was
danger they were to come back and call a
meeting of the settlers. Both had good
blooded horses, and they soon arrived at
Fair Haven, where they found the people
greatly excited, for a messenger with dis-
patches for Governor Ramsey had just arrived from the seat of war bringing information that the Indians and soldiers
had met in battle, and that a vast horde of
savages were butchering the inhabitants,
burning and torturing their captives, and
committing the most atrocious cruelties
ever known in the annals of savage warfare. They were sweeping everything before them, were coming our way, and unless checked we might expect them to
reach us in from 36 to 48 hours. They had
heard enough. The fearful thought that
their homes, their wives and children were
soon to be at the mercy of blood thirsty
savages, was enough to appal the stoutest
heart. Our town was so situated that it
would undoubtedly receive the first and
most furious shock of the advancing horde
of inhuman monsters.

WARNING THE SETTLERS.

It was then three o'clock p. m. The
settlers of Maine Prairie must be warned
to prepare to meet and repulse the foe.
There was no talk of seeking safety in
flight. We had a little band of 30 or 40
pioneers who could handle a gun who did
not propose to be driven from their homes
Wheeling their horses around, the two
couriers started back to warn the people

of their peril. Faster and faster they
urged their spirited horses, and as they
reached the settlement each took different routes stopping at each house just
long enough to tell them to be at
Spaulding's blacksmith shop at six p. m.,
to take measures against the Indians. The
blood and foam-covered sides, and heaving
flanks of their horses, carried conviction
to the settlers that prompt action was
necessary. At six o'clock the two couriers
dashed up to the blacksmith shop, both
horses and riders nearly exhausted. They
had personally warned each family, or
sent them word, and each had ridden over
thirty miles in three hours. Nearly every
man in town was there. The meeting was
called to order, and after fully discussing
the situation, it was unanimously decided
to stay and

FIGHT THE INDIANS

if they should attack us. An organization
was effected by choosing R. F. Adley
Captain, F. H. Dam, D. W. Fowler, E.
H. Atwood and Joseph Eaton were given
the title of 1st, 2d, 3d and 4th lieutenants;
R. F. Adley, F. H and Joseph Dam were
chosen a committee on fortifications, and
A. B. Greely was chosen commissary; F.
M. Kimball, Wm. H. Heywood and Alex
Spaulding were chosen as 1st, 2d and 3d
sergeants.

Every man was to come out the next
morning with teams, wagons and other
tools and meet at the blacksmith shop,
(which was near the center, and com-
manded a view of nearly all the prairie)
for the purpose of building a fort. James
Jenks and F. H. Dam were chosen to su-
pervise the building.

BUILDING A BLOCK HOUSE.

Early the next morning nearly every
man was on hand. A site just south of
the present Methodist church was chosen
for a fort. All day long men worked with
eager haste to erect an inclosure capable
of holding their families in case of an attack. The fort was forty feet square, made
by standing a double row of tamarack logs
on end close together. They were sixteen

feet above ground and two feet in the ground, all roofed in, making it when finally finished, three stories high. Timbers were run out under the eaves at two corners and bullet proof rifle pits were built capable of holding three or four rifle men, to protect the sides of the fort. House and barn logs, fence rails, barn timbers, bridge timber, wherever found, was taken with or without leave, but generally it was freely donated.

All that and the following day the men worked like beavers, but toward night of the second day, no fresh news coming in from the scene of Indian depredations, many began to doubt the danger, and the idea began to prevail that they had not secured sufficient evidence to warrant them in going to such an outlay. Some did not propose to do any more work on the fort until there was more proof of danger. The next morning only about half the men came back to work, the others went to harvesting their grain. Those working upon the fort had succeeded in getting the sides up when about four o'clock p. m. a courier arrived with the

STARTLING INTELLIGENCE

that the Indians had attacked the little settlement of Paynesville the night before and had massacred all the inhabitants and had perpetrated all the harrowing atrocities usually indulged in by savages. As Paynesville was but 22 or 23 miles from Maine Prairie, it was believed that the whole force of Indians would be upon us before morning. The reception of the startling news that the savages were so near at hand, and might even then be re-enacting the same fearful slaughter among their own families in the outskirts of the town created for awhile the utmost confusion and panic. A vote was immediately taken to get all the women and children together as soon as possible and start for St. Cloud. But the cool heads of R. F. Adley, Wm. L. Heywood, F. H. Dam, E. H. Atwood, James Jenks, A. B. Greely and others, showed them the danger of a long exposed line of teams going through the brush and

timber to St. Cloud, where a few Indians could kill the whole of them without danger to themselves. Another vote was taken, and it was agreed to bring all the women and children to the fort, place them in the stockade and the men guard the outside. It was then nearly five o'clock. There was not a moment to be lost. Those living at a distance whose houses were surrounded with timber, feared that their families might be the first victims of the relentless savages. This caused them to make all haste possible, and when they found their loved ones safe their hearts were full of thankfulness. Hastily selecting such articles of clothing and provision as were actually necessary, they hastened to a place of safety, admonished by the sinking sun. Swift couriers had been sent out and all had been warned of the impending danger.

GATHERING IN THE BLOCK HOUSE.

Soon after sundown the settlers and their families began to arrive at the fort. Capt. Adley and a part of the officers were kept busy making arrangements for the women and children, while others were equally active in fortifying and placing out pickets to prevent a surprise.

MILITARY PREPARATIONS FOR DEFENSE.

There were three houses near the fort (which was not yet roofed in,) in which the women and children were placed. Pass words were given out and orders given that no one was allowed outside the picket line. A few mounted pickets were sent out a mile or so with orders to dismount and listen with their ears to the ground. Upon the approach of danger they were to fire their guns and ride for the fort. Few if any men slept that night. It was believed that the Indians would attack us before morning. A few men worked all night long in building up breast works. Boxes, trunks and anything that could be found were used and before morning a fairly good breast work had been erected on four sides of the fort. Each man's arms were carefully examined and nothing was left undone that could be done to prepare for a conflict with the Indians. So the night passed and the morning came. After a hasty breakfast all went to work to finish the fort.

It was Sunday, and in the afternoon Elder Brooks preached a sermon in the stockade. Then work was resumed and by night the sides of the fort were considered bullet-proof and many of the families moved in. Many had ventured home and brought back supplies. That night, after carefully placing out a strong line of pickets and a few mounted ones, nearly all the rest, overcome by fatigue, had fallen asleep. About midnight a shot rang out upon the still night air from one of the mounted pickets a mile to the south, followed by the clatter of a horse coming with headlong speed. The alarm was given, the men sprang to their arms and quickly formed in line. A lieutenant, with nine men, was sent to each of the four breast works with orders to hold them at all hazards. There was no confusion. Orders were given and executed quickly, and, ere the arrival of the mounted picket, we were fully prepared to receive the foe with a force of ten men at each breast work and the captain with a small reserve in the center. Just then the horseman, A. D. Guptil came up and reported that he saw what he took to be an Indian partly emerge from the brush, and had shot at him and then started for the fort, but had gone but a few rods when he heard a horse whinney and thought it more than likely that it was a stray horse. A small party immediately started back to cautiously reconoiter, and found the object shot at to be a colt belonging to Orlen Farwell. It was slightly wounded in the leg. Mr. Farwell congratulated the picket upon his coolness. Then the sleepy and exhausted men sank down again to gain a little rest.

THE BRAVE WOMEN OF 1862.

The next day the work on the fort was resumed. While the men were busy, the women were not idle. There was but little ammunition in the town, but what there was was put into the general fund and the woman were busy making it up into cartidges. All the lead and pewter that could be found they manufactured into bullets and heavy shot. Bandages and lint were prepared. The commissary stocked the fort with.

PROVISIONS FOR A SIEGE.

Barrels were filled with water and placed into the fort, and lumber was prepared to curb a well inside in case of need. Teams were sent to St. Cloud for lumber and shingles for the fort. H. P. Bennett the gunsmith was kept busy fixing up old guns. No one was idle, for it was believed that the danger was imminent. Rumors of Indian depredations reached us daily, and many believed that they would be upon us before another sunrise.

THE MEN RECEIVE ORDERS.

Before night the men were assembled together and instructed how to act in case of an attack, when and where to assemble on the first alarm. None were allowed outside the lines. The countersign was given out, and a double line of pickets stationed around the fort. Every gun was carefully examined, and ammunition given out. Then those not on duty lay down to rest, with loaded guns and ammunition at their side. The pickets were changed at midnight. Several of the officers never retired, but kept a keen watch, listening to catch the first and faintest sound of an approaching foe. The night passed with no alarm, and next day the work on the fort was pushed ahead, with all vigor possible. The shingles had come and the roof and floors for the second and third stories were hurried forward.

STILL WAITING THE DREADED ATTACK.

Another day passed, rumors of the terrible fighting between settlers and Indians to the south and west of us were heard daily. Every precaution was taken to guard the loved ones. Pistols and knives were given to women with the command that they never allow themselves to be taken captive alive by the Indians. Most of the women and children now slept in the fort. The next day the roofs and floors were finished and each family was allotted a sleeping space. The dividing partition between families consisted often of only a chalk mark upon the floor. These slender and inadequate partitions occasionally led to ludicrous and sometimes serious blunders. A weary guard who had been relieved of picket-duty at midnight, would quietly enter the fort and relying upon his knowledge of the location of his own family's allotted space upon the second floor, would undertake to find it in the dark. The next morning's light might find him located two or three blocks away from his own, and in the vicinity of some other man's wife. It sometimes took a long time to satisfactorily explain to his wife and the woman's husband, just how the mistake occured. Little shanties to cook in were erected 40 to 60 rods from the fort and were occupied by one, two or more families during the day.

A COMMON INCIDENT.

About this time a strange woman was seen not far off calling for some of the women to come to her. They found her to be a Swede girl whose family, father, mother, brothers and sisters had been butchered and tortured before her eyes, and she had been taken captive by two lustful savages who had kept her for two or three days abusing her in the most horrible and brutal manner. Her clothing had been nearly all torn from her. She had succeeded in escaping from her fearful bondage and had wandered in an almost nude condition until we saw her. Our women clothed her and kindly cared for her until her strength returned, then sent her on to Clearwater, where she expected to find friends.

INDIANS IN SIGHT.

That night, just before dark, Mr. Stone, who had come down with his family from near Sauk Center, saw four Indians skulking among the willows near the lake, about eighty rods distant. Stone immediately reported the discovery to E. H. Atwood, one of the officers, Drill Sergeant F. H.

Dam, was ordered to immediately get all men in line and drill them, and have their arms inspected. The band of men with fife and drum made quite an imposing spectacle. A meeting of the women was called in the fort. Thus without any confusion all the women were gathered safely into the fort, and the men informed of the discovery of the Indians, and that we might expect an attack some time during the night. A strong picket line was put out, with orders to watch for Indians.

SKIRMISH ON THE PICKET LINE.

About nine o'clock the stillness of the night was broken by the reports of several shots on the picket line. It was then believed that the long looked for battle was about to begin. The orders of Capt. Adley ould be heard calling the men to rally around the fort. Lieutenant Atwood hastened to the picket line to assist in holding the Indians in check. He found the picket, Redman Field, bravely loading his gun. An Indian had crawled up through the grass to within three rods of Field and then fired, the shot fortunately striking the ground at his feet. Quick as possible Field, like a true veteran, had a bead on the Indian and fired. He sprang into the air and diappeared in the dark. Richard Vandervoort was the next to re-enforce the picket line, and his keen eye soon detected a dark object in the grass. As no one was allowed outside the lines, it was believed to be an Indian, and Vandervoort fired at it. When the smoke cleared away the object was gone. Not knowing what game the Indians were up to, the men slept with their arms by their sides, ready for immediate use. The next morning the trail where the Indians had wormed their way through the grass was easily seen.

SAVING THE CROPS.

During all this time a large part of the wheat and oats were standing uncut in the fields exposed to the destruction of the elements, which caused the grain to lodge. So, just as soon as the fort was completed, the men went out in small parties to harvest their grain, always keeping one or two men on the watch for the foe, each harvester keeping near his gun. As men were scarce several girls assisted by driving the reapers.

By this time, our numbers had been increased by additions from families further west. Among the number was Mr. Robert Wheeler and wife, and daughters Nellie and Lidia, Mr Stone and wife and son Frank and daughter Ella, and Wm. Westover from near Sauk Center.

One morning a party of nine men went to harvest E. H. Atwood's grain. Mrs. Thos. B. Standley volunteered to go to the house and cook the dinner. The house was situated in the edge of the timber. Every precaution was taken to prevent a surprise. Two men were placed on guard and every one kept his gun near him.

SETTLERS ATTACKED ON THE ROAD.

Messrs. Stone, Wheeler and Westover had decided to return to their homes, and about ten o'clock passed Atwood's house with an ox team and their families. About an hour after they had passed heavy and rapid firing was heard in the direction which they had taken. As the guns sounded like Indian guns, there was some uneasiness felt and just as the men were going to dinner Westover was seen coming running at his utmost speed. He was nearly exhausted and said that they were going along through the brush one and a half miles west of Pearl Lake, Wheeler a few rods ahead of the team, Stone just back of the wagon and he a little further back, when just as they came to the foot of a hill three Indians were seen dodging behind the bushes near the road and one of them rose up, but two or three rods off, and fired at Wheeler, but missed him. Wheeler returned the fire, and the Indian dropped behind the brush. Stone sprang forward just in time to see a naked savage taking deadly aim at Wheeler from behind a clump of bushes. His naked left side was exposed and Stone put in a charge of buck shot "where it did the most good." The Indian fell to the

ground without a groan and the other Indians fled. The wagon was turned around and they ran their oxen back a mile and a half to Mr. Watkins' house, where the oxen fell down from exhaustion. They had seen the Indians running their ponies to get ahead of them and cut off their retreat, but they had failed, and had come out into the road a little behind them. Stone and Wheeler and their families took refuge in the Watkins house and Westover had come on to our place for help. From the boldness of the attack, it was thought there were quite a number of Indians. No time was to be lost if we would save the besieged ones. Orders were rapidly given and quickly executed. A. S. Greely was ordered to hitch his team to a wagon and take Mrs. Standly to the fort with all possible speed. One or two other men were sent to warn other parties, who were harvesting in other places, and scouts were sent out to prevent a surprise. Mrs. Standly was informed of the situation and danger, and that the men were going to rescue the besieged people, and that she was to get into the wagon and go to the fort in haste, but she insisted that as dinner was all ready we should eat before going. It was argued that the danger was imminent, that even now there was danger of our being surrounded by the savages, or that the women and children might be captured if we delayed. She still insisted that we would be half sick if we went "trapesing off there without our dinner," and that the beans would all be cold and mussed up. Just then hearing firing in the direction of the Watkins house she was persuaded to go. The rest of the party, six or seven in number, started for the rescue. The Indians fled upon their approach. The oxen were found alive and able to travel, and were hurriedly started for the fort, with the women and children, and guarded out of the timber by the whole force. Five then started to rescue Mr. A. Maservey, John White and H. Clark, who were harvesting a small field west of M. Greely's The Indians had been seen on their ponies near this field. The field was found deserted, the horses gone, and appearances indicated that the place had been raided. While cautiously reconnoitering the place, Atwood saw a bald head and red face peering around the corner of the old log house. Taking it for the head of an Indian he took aim and was just pulling the trigger, when he discovered his mistake. It was A. Maservey's head. It was a narrow escape. The men were taking their after dinner nap and knew nothing of their danger. The whole party then started for the dead or wounded Indian that Stone had shot, and were soon joined by about 20 from the fort. When the watchmen on the fort saw A. S. Greely running his horses to the fort he raised the alarm flag and fired the signal guns. The harvesters came pouring in from all directions and when they heard of the peril of their comrades, hastened forward to their assistance, the party were so close upon the retreating Indians that they had barely time to snatch their dead or wounded comrade and escape, leaving, where he had fallen, a new bed cord, an oil cloth gun cover, a woman's shawl, a white clean new woolen bed blanket and an old smoked Indian blanket. Their trail was followed over the hills a mile or more and lost. The party returned to the fort with appetites that could relish beans, even if they were cold and all mussed up. Thus far the Indians had found our people alert and watchful, brave and ready on the instant. Contious and crafty as the Indians were, It is untoubtedly due to our attitude, that the savages were deterred from making any formidable raid upon our settlement. Thus we were saved from the fate of many other sections.

F. H. DAM RIDES TO ST PAUL.

We had but few guns and but little ammunition. F. H. Dam volunteered to go to St. Paul and endeavor to procure some guns and powder and shot from the government. He had John Farwell's fast horse, and made the trip of 150 miles in about 36 hours, braving the dangers of driving through alone in the night from Clearwater. The few old muskets and ammunition that he could get were gladly received. After that John Farwell drove to St. Paul and returned with more old muskets and ammunition. The wonderful and vigorous kick which these old muskets could exert made it equally dangerous to be at either end when they were fired off. But they had bayonets on them and looked formidable.

The next year John White was hunting for a lost cow and had one of these kicking government muskets. Getting up on a high log for a better view, he discovered a black bear but a few rods away. Bruin saw him at the same time and raised up on his hind legs. White took good aim and fired. The gun kicked him heels over head and the last he saw of the bear he was performing a similar acrobatic feat.

WILLMOTT MAYBEE AND COMRADES KILLED.

There was a small settlement at Mannanah, 22 miles west of Maine Prairie, of four or five families. Upon the first alarm they had all fled to safer places, some to Clearwater and some to other places. After remaining a few days a party of ten or fifteen men thought there was no danger and returned to get supplies of provisions and other goods and to look after their stock. They were urged not to go, as it was believed to be a dangerous undertaking. But they had no fear. When they arrived near their homes two of their number, Thomas Ryckman and Chauncy Willson left the wagon to look after some cattle. Mr. Willmot Maybee, Lyman Howe and Joseph Page were in the two-horse wagon Mr. Maybee was driving, and Philip Deck was driving a one horse rig.

Willson and Ryckman were about 80 rods distant, when just as the party drove up to their house imagine their horror to see a party of Indians rise up from behind a pile of lumber and shoot and kill the four men in the wagons. These two men on foot sprang into the timber with the Indians in close pursuit. They succeeded in escaping from their persuers and started for Maine Prairie Fort where they arrived almost bereft of their senses, bare headed and bare footed. They were brave men, but the horror of seeing their friends killed and mangled, and fearing every moment that they might be overtaken by the savages whom they imagined were pursuing them during their long flight, had completely prostrated them.

The balance of the party coming up later discovered the dead bodies of their comrades and started at once for Forest City, not waiting to investigate. They put in a horrowing night wading through marshes and brush, not daring to keep the road for fear of meeting Indians. They reached the City the next morning in a deplorable condition. A party of men went right back and found all except Maybee who was found two months later by a soldier. Mr. Howe had been scalped and Mr. Page's throat was cut from ear to ear. The others were not mutulated. Mr. Ryckman is now one of Meeker county's most prosperous farmers and is living at Union Grove. But he will never forget his thrilling experience at Mannanah, Aug. 26, 1862.

This incident caused us to redouble our precautions at the fort. From many signs seen and heard it was believed that our movements were closely watched by our savage foe from the surrounding hills, but finding us always on the alert, brave and ready to dash out whenever there was a foe or sign of a foe in sight, and a match for them in caution and strategy, they dared not to molest us. The brave stand made by these resolute men undoubtedly had its influence in holding in check the savages.

WHAT THE LOOKOUT FOUND.

A little incident that occurred about this time still farther strengthened them in the belief that our movements were being watched by the Indians. R. M. Vandervoort was appointed to keep a lookout from the top of the fort during the day with a telescope to guard against a surprise by the Indians. He faithfully filled that responsible position for three weeks. One day be engaged a substitute to fill his place while he took a vacation, and went into the timber near Cornelian lake for wild plums. He had not proceeded far when he discovered a small pile of ashes. As they looked fresh he was somewhat startled. Thrusting his hand into them he discovered that there was fire, and believing that the fire had been built by an Indian and fearing he might then be near and probably drawing a bead on him, he claims that he made the best time on record in his flight to the fort.

GETTING AMMUNITION AT ST. CLOUD.

It was understood at St. Cloud that a courier would be sent through from the prairie each way unless surrounded by the foe. It was brush and timber nearly all the way and the messenger could easily be shot by an unseen savage. The next morning D. A. Hoyt, E. H. Atwood and H. P. Bennett volunteered to go through to St. Cloud. It was one of the darkest periods of the outbreak. James Jenks offered them his ponies. Mr. Jenks was one of those big hearted, whole souled men often found on the frontier. These ponies were thoroughly disgusted with life in this world, and it required some very weighty argument, and unscriptural language, besides the vigorous application of a three-quarter inch brad, to induce them to go faster than a walk. The citizens of St. Cloud were found badly frightened and many leaving for the east. The were fearful that the Chippewas would be down upon them. General H. Z. Mitchell presented Atwood with two sacks of buck shot and a can of powder. We were in great need of ammunition and were glad to get these supplies for the fort. It was near midnight when the party reached the prairie on their return.

TWO FALSE ALARMS.

They found the men at the fort all under arms and a double line of pickets on guard. Joseph Watkins, and Mr. and Mrs. J. H. Noyes had gone out to R. F. Adley's house to sleep. It was against the orders of the captain to leave the fort at night without leave. No one knew that anyone was outside the fort. Near midnight Watkins saw through the window what he took to be three Indians on ponies near the house. Hastily taking his gun and awakening Mr. Noyes he was ready to give them a warm reception. But they had mysteriously disappeared. He immediately gave the alarm by firing the danger signal. The fort was aroused, but as no one knew of anyone being outside of the lines, it was thought to be a decoy. After firing the danger signal, several times Watkins came to the fort and reported his discovery. Several went down with a buggy and brought Mrs. Noyes to the fort. It proved to be three stray colts that were taken for Indians.

The second day after this scare, a party of men from St. Cloud, who had been out beyond Forest City to bury some of their countrymen, who had been murdered by the Sioux, were returning home. When about one and a half miles from the fort in the timber they thoughtlessly began firing off their guns to clean them. Hearing the firing at the fort it was thought that the Indians were attacking the whites. Then there was mounting in hot haste and swiftly forming, a strong force was soon upon the spot ready for action, but they discovered their mistake before any blood was shed.

THE ATTACK ON FOREST CITY.

No fresh rumors of Indian depredations had been heard for a day or two, and the men were somewhat relaxing the usual vigilance and were hoping that "the cruel war was o'er," when just before night a messenger came through from Forest City, 16 miles southwest of us, with word that their fort had been attacked the night before by a band of Sioux and several had been killed and the rest compelled to remain in the fort and see the Indians harness their horses to wagons, load them

with plunder and go off. At this fort there was a company of cavalry and about one hundred and fifty armed citizens. As we had but forty or fifty men at our fort with but little ammunition and very inferior arms, we felt that our position was critical.

Every man was called in, arms examined and everything done that could be done to prepare for the worst. The wagons were rendered useless by taking off and hiding the nuts and the horses were turned loose in a large pasture There was little sleep that night. From the actions of the dogs, it was thought they heard or smelled Indians. They sniffed the air to the west and barked continually. One of our men burning with a desire to avenge the wrongs and cruelties that he had seen and heard of felt a strong desire to shoot and scalp an Indian. So intense was this passion that he went to the picket on the west and told him he was going to reconnoiter for a scalp. Carefully loading his gun, with pistol and knife in his belt, he began crawling off into the darkness listening with ear to the ground then advancing, then listening and peering through the darkness often imagining that he could hear the approach of the crafty foe or that some dark object in the grass might be a skulking savage, until after hours of patient search he crawled back greatly disappointed. The Indians were not be caught napping. The next day the fortifications were strenghtened by building a breast work all around them and just outside of this a deep ditch or moat was dug 10 feet deep and 10 feet wide. Our horses were placed in this at night. We now felt that we could hold our fort against five hundred savages and did not need so many pickets. All slept in the fort nights, except those who where out as pickets or to go out at midnight. These slept in the blacksmith shop.

INDIANS DRIVEN OFF BY TROOPS.

Soon after the raid on Forest City, the Indians were driven back by the State and United States troops, and the settlers began to feel safer, although occasional signs were seen that would indicate that there were a few savages skulking around, who would murder whenever they could. A few began to leave the fort and go to their homes.

ATTACKED BY AN INDIAN.

Old Mr. Field, his son and daughter, went to their home one morning, and in the afternoon the daughter went into the brush near by to pick plums. A painted warrior rose up near her and sprang for her. She screamed and ran for the house the Indian in close pursuit. Just as she reached the edge of the brush he caught her dress by one hand and struck her with a knife with the other hand. She tore loose, and as her father and brother, hearing her screams, had come to her assistance, the Indian retreated. The wound received was on her arm and not very deep. She was brought to the fort, but was prostrated for some time from the shock.

WATER MELON BRIGADE.

This time a number of young men, with a man calling himself "Captain," came to the fort, and confiscated some horses, grain and provisions, in the name of the State or some other authority. They might have been of great help to the people, but their undesciplined actions and wild behavior made them obnoxious. They were called the "Water Melon Brigade," on account of their many raids upon the water melon patches.

RETURNED TO THEIR HOMES.

Gradually the people sought their homes, but some stayed at the fort until cold weather, when all left, and the usual routine of parties, lectures, meetings, surprise parties and donations followed each other in rapid succession. It must not be inferred from this fact that life was one of sad and fearful foreboding. There were many occasions of merriment; many laughable incidents, many pleasant hours, and, among the younger lads and lassies, many a tender look and action that were the first seeds that soon ripened into a closer union of soul to soul. No doubt, the peril that surrounded them made many a young man vow to sell his life dearly, should it ever be necessary, in defense of the young lady walking by his side; and the proud bearing and brave demeanor of her young escort would tend to soften the heart of the most obdurate maiden. Oh, there is nothing like a common danger, and a common cause to bring the hearts of brave men and women to beat in unison. But, alas for the fickleness of the human heart. It is believed that in more than one case, when the danger was over and the close associations were ended, that time, distance and other associations, gradually caused a coolness, then a final severing of the once united hearts.

A NEWSPAPER ITEM.

In the St. Cloud *Democrat*, of Sept. 4, 1862, under the head of "locals" appeared the following:

"As we go to press, this note is handed us. It is from a well known Maine Prairie citizen to his wife:

Dear Augusta: We were cutting our wheat yesterday, when a man came running saying they had started back to Cold Springs with three men, women and children in an ox team. When they had got a mile beyond John White's three Indians arose. One Indian fired at one of the men not more than twenty feet off, but missed him Each of the men fired, and one Indian dropped as though killed. Then the men turned the team around and run the oxen back to the Cutter house. The Indians trying to head them off, but did not succeed. Two of the men stayed with the women in the house, while the other came through and told me. We took a wagon and went over and got the family to a safe place, and then went up to find the dead Indian. We found two blankets, a shawl, a bed cord and gun cover, and some blood, but no Indian. We had an alarm this morning about 4 o'clock. I have no time for particulars.   E. H. ATWOOD.

THE WINTER OF 1862-3.

On account of the trouble with the Indians, quite a percentage of the crop of 1862 was lost or damaged, and it was very late in the fall before the grain was all secured. Although the settlers had plenty to eat, still, on account of their losses and the hard times, they had to economize in every possible way during the winter of

1862-3. Tea, coffee and sugar were luxuries that but few could indulge in. Home grown tobacco was largely used as a substitute for that sold in the stores. A new suit of store clothes on a person at church would attract so much attention that the fervent words of the minister had but little effect upon the congregation. The woman with a brand new calico dress was generally greeted with a coldness by her less fortunate sisters that made her wish that she had worn her old dress. Many of the more nervous people were still timid, fearing that the Indians might come back and do damage. But, spring came, and it was believed that there would be no more trouble with them.

SIGNS OF INDIANS AGAIN.

Soon, however, signs, showing that small parties of Indians were lurking around, were frequently met with. Mr. Goodner found in a patch of brush not far from his house fresh signs where apparently several savages had cleared out a space in the patch where they could lay concealed and watch what was going on around them. They had undoubtedly been making bridles out of raw-hide for clippings and strips of untanned hide had been left on the ground where they had lain. It was supposed that their object was to steal horses, but it was believed that they would not hesitate to shoot a white person whenever they could safely do so. Several persons had been shot at by unseen foes, and a few killed or wounded in the Big Woods to the south. Great uneasiness was felt by the people. The men mostly went armed and the women were careful about keeping the doors fastened. Finally the State organized a

COMPANY OF SCOUTS

and about three were detailed to each town for the purpose of patroling the town, and to be ready to concentrate at any threatened point. These scouts were of great benefit in allaying the fears of the citizens. They were alert, and investigated many alarms and scares, which often proved groundless, but which occasionally clearly indicated that Indians were around. If a man found himself in the vicinity of Indians, or had any reason to believe that there was danger of his coming in contact with them, when he was unarmed, it was considered wise and proper to seek safety with all possible speed.

AN AMUSING INCIDENT.

One instance of a causeless panic occurred when David Goodner and M. V. Greely went after wild plums. They entered a large plum thicket from opposite sides at the same time. Each heard the other, and by stooping down and looking under the brush they could see the legs of the other, and the two front and two hind feet of their horses. They could not see high enough to see the bodies of the men or horses. In their excitement, each mistook the other party for at least three Indians, and both sprang upon their horses and rode for their lives in opposite directions, and spread the news that they had seen Indians. Of course there was but little sleep in the neighborhood that night. Guns were carefully loaded and ammunition brought out and all precautions taken to guard against any raid the Indians might make. A careful investigation the next morning revealed the true facts in the case. Every few days some such an alarm would be given in some part of the town. Many, upon investigation, proved groundless. Others would show that Indians were around and the settlers did not know at what moment they might be the victim of a crafty foe that was able to lay in wait for days to get a shot at a white man.

LITTLE CROW'S LAST DITCH.

A large body of troops had driven the main body of Indians back into the Bad Lands of the Dakotas the fall before, but Little Crow, a celebrated Sioux chief, his son, and a few others had passed through the lines and returned to the settlements to steal horses, and avenge certain wrongs. But the tragic death of Little Crow; the narrow escape of his son; the disastrous results to the three Indians that stole Block's horses, as well as the failure of those Indians who stole Mr. King's horses, but which they had to relinquish, so disheartened them that they soon sought safety among their people on the western plains. Little Crow's son was soon captured on the plains, and brought back by Geo. Sibley in the fall of 1863. They camped on the east side of the river, and many St. Cloud people visited the tent of of Little Crow's son.

THE DROUTH OF 1863.

The summer of 1863 will long be remembered for the protracted drouth. There was hardly any rain after the spring crops were sown until they were harvested, consequently the crops were light.

"ATWOOD'S SCHOOL."

In the winter of 1863-4 E. H. Atwood taught a term of school in the school house in district No. 29, called the Stanly district. The house was a mere shell, and it was impossible to keep warm. There was no furniture except a desk or two and benches to sit on, but the scholars were all eager to get an education and studied hard while their feet ached with the cold. They could rest their tired eyes occasionally by looking out doors, through wide cracks in the walls of the building. A few of the names of those who attended that school were "D. B.," Roger, Plum and Joseph Stanly, Luellen and John French, two daughters, Helen and Mandy, and Herbert, son of Dudley French, Fred and Mabel Hamilton, and his sister, now Mrs. Albert Guptil, Bertha Scribner, her brother Frank Frank, Albert Guptil, Fred Greely, and his sister, the late Mrs. E. G. Hicks, Thos. O. Spaulding, Mrs. Horace Greely, Nellie Kimball, and her brother Gilbert, Velora and Lydia Adley, and Osgood, their brother, Ada A. Dam, Charles and Hattie Wood, Bertha Clark, Martin F. Greely, and Alberton Whitney, (who afterwards died in a southern hospital.) There were others whose names cannot be recalled just now. No one thought when he saw that

group of boys studying on those poor benches, with cold feet, their noses red, and lips purple with the cold, or when they were declaiming their little pieces, or speaking their dialogues, at spelling school, that when they grew up to manhood, the clarion voices of a number of them would be heard harranguing the assembled wisdom of the State in the Legislative halls, for hours at a time on the mighty questions of the period, or assisting by voice and vote in enacting laws for the protection of the people of the State, against gigantic monopolies. Nearly all of them have been called to fill some responsible public position at some times of their lives.

A LYCEUM ORGANIZED.

During the winter there would be a spelling school about every two weeks. At the close of spelling there would be dialogues and declamations. The improvement in this line was rapid and at the last one held on the 26th of Feb., 1864, the house was crowded full and the audience became so enthusiastic that it was proposed then and there to organize a lyceum and choose officers. Accordingly J. R. Watkins was chosen President; J. H. French, vice-President; E. H. Atwood, Secretary, and D. S. French, Treasurer. They then adjourned to meet in the school house near where the Baptist church now stands, on the 2nd of March. This second meeting was very interesting, although it was a new thing, and but a few were willing to take hold and do their part. R. F. Adley, D. B. Standley and E. H. Atwood were appointed a committee to draft a constitution and by-laws for the government of the lyceum and a library. At a regular meeting, March 11th, the constitution and by-laws were adopted, and the following officers were elected: J. R. Watkins, president; J. H. French and Alex. Spaulding, vice presidents; S. Young, secretary; W. L. Heywood, treasurer; R. F. Adley, librarian. The question debated at this meeting was:

Resolved, That a prohibitory liquor law is beneficial to the temperance cause.

The speakers in the affirmative were D. A. Hoyt, E. H. Atwood and A. B. Greely; in the negative were S. Young, J. R. Watkins and Alex. Spaulding.

There was increased interest manifested in the Lyceum during the summer. On the 2d of December, 1864, the first number of the "Maine Prairie *Gem*" was published by the members, Mrs. E H. Atwood, being editress? It was a fine paper and a decided success. Meetings were held every two weeks during the winter of 1864-5.

FOURTH OF JULY CELEBRATION.

At the meeting of June 16, 1865, it was decided to have a big celebration in the Farwell grove on the 4th of July, and the following committees were appointed:

Committee on Flags and Arrangements—O. Farwell, T. O. Spaulding, S. Young, D. G. Reefe.

Committee on Lumber—J. E. Young and R. F. Adley.

Committee on Speakers—A. B. Greely and R. F. Adley.

Committee on Toasts—E. H. Atwood.

Committee on Water—Joseph Stanley.

Committee on Ice—R. F. Adley.

Committee on Guess Cake—Mrs. O. Farwell.

Committee on Tables—Mrs J. Dam, Mrs. O. Farwell, Mrs. S. Young, Mrs. M. Patten, Mrs. E. H. Atwood, Miss P. Field.

Committee on Ring Cake—Mrs . A. B. Greely.

Committee on Post Office—Miss A. Boobar.

Committee on Singing—Mrs. Strout, Mrs. Fowler, Mrs. Neal, Miss L. Greely, Mr. D. A. Roberts, E. H Atwood, D. S. French and A. F. Perkins.

Committee on Minister's Cake—Mrs. E. H. Atwood.

The celebration on the Fourth was a grand affair. A. B. Curry, of St. Cloud, delivered the oration. There was an immense number of people present not only from our own town, but from all the adjoining towns. There was good speaking, good music and a good dinner. The society cleared about $125. The ring cake sold for $10. The guess cake $2 90. The lemonade stand cleared $13.50. Post office $26.20. But the minister's cake created the most interest. It was to be donated to the clergyman who received the most votes. The votes cost five cents each, and any person could vote as many times as he wished at that price. There were 928 votes cast. The cake brought $46.40.

The library had 122 volumes that fall. A course of five lectures and exhibitions were given that winter. The proceeds were used to get lumber for a stage and curtains and scenery, and to defray expenses of getting the speakers out there. The balance of the money was used to buy books for the library and pay the librarian. The Lyceum was kept up in first class shape for 4 or 5 years. Then on account of sickness and other causes, there were but few meetings until the fall of 1871, when there was a revival of the Lyceum. A new constitution and by-laws were adopted and there was much interest taken in the society. A course of lectures was arranged and exhibitions were given. These exhibitions consisted of a one or two act plays, being sometimes a farce, at other times a comedy, and at rare intervals a tragedy was attempted. Besides this there would be a paper, the Prairie *Gem*, filled with original productions from the members. This would be followed by recitations and dialogues. At the next meeting there would be a lecture followed by music and a short play. A debate would be had occasionally. Generally there would be a lecture, then in two weeks an exhibition, followed in two weeks by a debate. Among the lecturers was the Hon. D B Searle, then a slim, quiet young man. C. C. Andrews gave us a lecture, taking Shakespeare's Falstaff as a subject. Several other St. Cloud lawyers and ministers lectured before the society. Many of the best members of the society had either moved away or passed over the silent river. It was hoped that the young and rising generation would come forward and fill the places of the old and feeble and carry on the Lyceum with its usual vigor, but for various causes it languished and there were but few meetings held from the spring of 1872 until the spring of 1873 when a special meeting was called and it was voted to sell the books and fixtures belonging to the library at public auction. This was very unfortunate. The library contained at least 200 volumes and had been very largely patronized and been of inestimable value to the early settlers by furnishing them the use of such a fine set of books, but according to the vote on the 6th of June, 1873, this splendid library of about 200 books with book case lamps, curtains, lumber, &c., were sold and scattered over the town. The amount realized was only $40 25. The Lyceum was thus broken up never to meet again.

It was the fond hope of the older members of the society that the younger people of th- Prairie, when they had grown up, would take hold of the work and carry the Lyceum along, gradually improving the work and increasing the library and acquiring a love for greater knowledge. It was with profound sorrow that the old members saw the labor of years scattered to the winds.

We trust that the young people of good old Maine Prairie who have lately organized a literary and debating society will take hold of the work and carry it forward and build up a magnificent literary society that will be known and honored throughout the state. Let it be a vast improvement upon the first one. The labor of carrying on the Lyceum in those early days was performed under many difficulties. The country was new and the people poor and scattered. But with all advantages that the youth now enjoy of excellent schools and cheap books, and with the assistance of the many talented leaders in the society, the brilliant future of your society is fully assured.

School district No. 32 of Maine Prairie was organized in 1861 and the first teacher was Miss Evelyn McKenney. The present school house was built in 1869. The present officers are Wm. L. Heywood, director; S. Young, treasurer; S. F. Brown, clerk.

The Kimball school district No. 80, was organized in 1869 and a school house was built in 1870. The first officers were: J.M. Kimball, T. J. Wiley and Michael Patten. The first teachers were Mary Wiley and Belle Wiley. This school house was moved into the village of Kimball, and in 1890 school district No. 147 was organized and a house built the same year. This last district embraced much of the territory of the old district. The first officers were W. W. Connor, Edwin Baker and Joseph Mason. The first teachers were Nellie Kimball, Celia Kimball and Emma Lytle.

IN THE DAYS OF 1864.

At the town meeting in April, 1864, it was "voted that a bounty of two (2) cents per head for squirrels and five (5) cents p r head for gophers be paid by the town. Voted that the Justices of the Peace, Chairman of Supervisors and Town Clerk be authorized to count all squirrels and gophers presented to them and give the bearer a receipt for them." As no money was voted to pay the bounty a special town meeting was called in June, and $135 voted to be raised for that purpose. The first year there was paid out in bounties for squirrels and gophers the sum of $181.30. In April, 1866, it was "voted to pay no more bounties for squirrels or gophers."

There were some funny articles written at the time about the results of this bounty business. It was required that only the tails of the animals need be brought to the officers to be counted. It was claimed that the boys often secured the tails and let the squirrels go, and that stump-tailed squirrels were very plentiful on the Prairie, and that as these tailless animals were not molested by the boys they in time became very tame and that by certain Darwinian laws of evolution and the survival of the fittest, and that while those animals with full caudal appendages were hunted, trapped and destroyed, those with little or no such appendage were free from persecution, and that as a natural consequence of the laws governing the survival of the fittest and of natural selection the tail of the squirrels under such conditions would gradually disappear and in time a race of tailless squirrels would take the place of those whose candle appendage had proved their ruin.

In July of this year there was a weekly mail route established from St. Cloud to Fair Haven by way of Maine Prairie. The mail came in from St Cloud Tuesday morning and returned the same day.

Alonzo Spaulding, of Maine Prairie, and Christina Langdon, of Clearwater, were married July 4, 1864.

MORE INDIANS AND SOME POLITICS.

During the summer the Indians had been troublesome in parts of the state. A raid by a party of Sioux had been made near Mankato and several whites were killed or wounded, and horses were stolen, and a freight train near Breckenridge had been attacked and a number killed and wounded. This caused more or less uneasiness, and a feeling of unrest. Politics ran high this summer and fall. It was the year in which the President was to be elected as well as congressmen and members of the legislature. Consequently there was great excitement in the political world. Lincoln was a candidate for re-election. Ignatius Donnelly was a candidate for Congress. Hon. H. C. Waite and E. H. Atwood were candidates for the State Legislature. Donnelly's course as acting Governor in the absence of Governor Ramsey had made him popular and when he came to St. Cloud Oct. 24, 1864, to make a political speech a large delegation from Maine Prairie came in to hear him. The front wagon carried a large American flag and a banner on which was inscribed: "Lincoln and Donnelly."

In the fall, of 1864, while Capt. Thos. E. Inman was out hunting, he was shot at by another hunter, who mistook him for a deer, the ball passing through his coat sleeve. A narrow escape.

THE BOYS IN BLUE RETURN.

A supper was given Dec. 26th, 1864, at the Farewell school house, to the returned soldiers. There was a large gathering. O. Farwell was chosen president of the meeting, and in an appropriate address gave the soldiers a hearty welcome, and touchingly alluded to those of their number whom death had taken while in the service of their country. Capt. Inman replied in behalf of the soldiers. It was a pleasant affair and will long be remembered by those present.

RAISING THE TOWN'S QUOTA.

President Lincoln was calling for more troops, and the officers of the town of Maine Prairie were endeavoring to ascertain whether the town would be called upon to furnish more volunteers, and if so to devise ways and means to fill the town's quota.

Alpheus Maservey, as chairman of the supervisors, and E. H. Atwood, as town clerk, labored diligently to see that justice was secured the town, and that all the volunteers from the town were properly accredited. Many towns were offering from $200 to $225 for volunteers to fill their quotas. In pursuance of a petition properly signed and delivered, a special town meeting was called to meet at the Farewell school house Jan 7th, 1865, to see if the voters would vote to raise sufficient money to hire volunteers to fill the town's quota. At this meeting it was voted that the supervisors be authorized to raise money for the purpose of hiring volunteers to fill the town's quota. Also that D. W. Fowler, D. A. Hoyt and E. H. Atwood act with the supervisors as a committee. This committee succeeded in hiring six volunteers for a total of $1,450. It was also voted that the supervisors be authorized to issue to all soldiers who had served two years, a town order of the amount of their tax for volunteer money now to be raised. The town bonds were sold at a discount of 15 cents on the dollar.

AS TO THE SIX VOLUNTEERS.

Of the six volunteers that were hired by the town, three of them, viz: Alberton Whitney, David Goodner and Thomas Falone, enlisted in the First Regiment Heavy Artillery, Feb. 2d, 1865, and were sent to Chattanooga, Tenn. Alberton Whitney died at that place April 23d, 1865. The other three, Albert Guptil, A. Clark and J. W. Clark enlisted Feb. 16, 1865, in Company E, 2d Regiment Cavalry, and were mustered out with the company and were discharged that fall with the company.

GREAT CELEBRATION JULY 4, 1865.

The splendid harvest of 1864, the promise of a bountiful yield this year, and above all else, the feeling that the long and bloody war of the rebellion was about over, and the expectation that the boys in blue would soon return to their homes, caused much joy and happiness among the citizens. In their gladness they concluded to celebrate the Fourth of July in a manner befitting the occasion, and as a consequence of this feeling arrangements were made for a monster picnic on the old picnic grounds, in the Farwell grove, on the shore of the beautiful Cornelian Lake. Never before or since has the shores of that lake seen such a gathering of happy people from that and surrounding towns. A. B. Curry, of St. Cloud, was the orator of the day. The Burbanks and many others from St. Cloud were there. Fair Haven, Lynden, and many other towns had large delegations present. The Maine Prairie and Fair Haven Glee Club sang the popular war songs of the times. The oration was excellent. The orator paid a great tribute to those who had left their homes and fought in defense of their country, and by their bravery and perserverance had saved the country from anarchy and ruin. Few eyes were dry when he feelingly alluded to those that had given up their lives in defense of their coun-

try. Some of the soldiers were present. Some of them had experienced all of the horrors of prison life in Andersonville, Libby, and other prisons, while others had been disabled from wounds. The happiness of the people seemed complete. It was a great relief to the people, when, after years of anxiety from short crops, from hard times, from Indian depredations, from doubts and fears regarding the safety of the country during the rebellion, and from the thoughts of the loved ones on Southern battle fields, that now, these was, every prospect that all of three causes either had disappeared, or soon would, and the future seemed to give promise of peace, plenty and happiness.

With the hardships and privations of early pioneer life forgotten, and with bright anticipations of a glorious future, the citizens of Maine Prairie started out anew for a higher realization of life.

This ends the present early history of Maine Prairie. We humbly ask the reader to be lenient and overlook its many imperfections.

KIMBALL, MAINE PRAIRIE.

Kimball is a thriving village in the southern part of the town with a present (1895) population of about 500. In 1886, the first houses were built in the townsite, and in 1891 the village was incorporated and G. R. Calkins, G. W. Beckman, J. W. Kennedy and E. Peck were elected the first officers. The "Soo" rail road runs past the town. There is a rich and fertile territory on all sides of the village, and the farmers find a good market for their produce at this point.

The M. E. Church of Kimball was organized in 1888, and the house built the same year. The first trustees were F. Driver, J. M. Kennedy and A. Spaulding. The first ministers were J. Kindred and W. Wilson.

The School District was organized in 1887 and a fine school house was built, 40 by 70 by feet. The first officers were E. Mayhew, J. B. McCann and E. A. Westcott, and the first teacher was Miss J. Leayton.

The present teachers are D. W. Spaulding and Mrs. E. Bullivant.

BIOGRAPHIES.

Following the historical portion of what has been written of the town, I will give short biographical sketches of some of its early pioneers, and those who have been more or less intimately connected with its history.

The lives of the men who establish and found a nation, or discover and settle a new country, and build up its communities, ever form an integral part of the history of the same. To the early pioneers of the town of Maine Prairie, the present generation of its people, and those which will follow, owe much. Anything connected with their lives must be of great interest, and, therefore, I have deemed it appropriate to append to the history of the "Prairie" brief biographical sketches of "the first settlers."

ARRIVALS IN 1856.

R. F. ADLEY.

R. F. Adley was born in Waterford, Maine, in 1819. In 1856, accompanied by his wife and daughters Lydia, Valora and Ella, and son Osgood, he arrived and settled on the Prairie, where he remained until 1870, when he moved to Otter Tail county. He died in 1885. Mr. Adley was prominent in the affairs of town and school, holding for a long time important offices in both. He was chosen captain of the Maine Prairie Guards during the Indian outbreak. He was one of the leading men who organized and carried on the Lyceum and Library.

GEORGE CLARK.

George Clark was born on Cape Cod in 1814, and came to Maine Prairie in 1856, and took a claim and operated it for about fifteen years, when he moved to Otter Tail county, where he died in 1884. His family consisted of his wife and son George A., and daughters Eliza and Bethie.

THOMAS CADWELL.

Thomas Cadwell was one of Stearns county's pioneers, arriving in the county in 1855, and settling on his claim in

Maine Prairie in 1857, with his wife. He was born in Madison county, New York, in 1832. In October, 1861, he enlisted in the 4th regiment, and after serving three years re-enlisted and served ten months as a veteran. Since returning to Maine Prairie at the close of the war, he has been engaged in farming ever since, except a short time when acting as a guard in the Reformatory.

F. H. DAM.

F. H. Dam was born in Enfield, Maine, in 1835. He took a claim on Maine Prairie, but spent much of his time for a number of years working at his trade in Minneapolis, afterwards establishing himself in business in St. Cloud. Since then, he has been so well known throughout the county that it is needless to add anything regarding his life. During the fort life on Maine Prairie in 1862, his coolness, bravery and knowledge of military tactics, were of inestimable value to the settlers during those perilous times. He was one of the officers, and drove through to St. Paul and procured arms and ammunition for those in the fort, when many brave men shrank from the dangerous undertaking.

JOSEPH DAM.

Joseph Dam was born in Cumberland, Maine, in 1830. In 1856, he arrived at Maine Prairie. His wife and only daughter, Ada A., joined him the next year. He took a claim joining his brother Hercules, and carried on his farm for eight or nine years. His wife died and he went to Dakota, where he has resided ever since. Mr. Dam was a quiet citizen, a good neighbor, charitable and kind hearted. His family were intelligent and well educated, and the community keenly felt their loss when they moved away.

HERCULES DAM.

Hercules Dam was born in Newfield, Maine, in 1806, and was one of the very first settlers on Maine Prairie, his wife being the first white woman on the Prairie. His son, F. H., and daughter Zelia, accompanied him to his new home. He built the first house and broke the first land in the town, and operated his farm until 1864, when he moved to St. Cloud. Mr. Dam was a man of great influence for good in the community, and his neighbors looked up to him for advice and counsel in spiritual as well as the more practical concerns of life. After the death of his wife in 1864, he returned to Maine Prairie and remained there a number of years, living with his daughter, Mrs. C. F. Hamilton. He was a leading member and deacon of the Baptist church.

ORLEN FARWELL.

Orlen Farwell was born in Compton, Canada. He moved to Boston, Massachusetts, where he resided fifteen years. In 1856, he arrived at Maine Prairie, and bought one-half interest of Moses Ireland in the townsite of Marysville. Returning to Boston, his wife and son, Quartus, accompanied him back to his new home. In 1858 he was appointed postmaster, being the first one in the town. The postoffice was established at Marysville. He served as justice of the peace for a number of years.

JOHN FARWELL.

John Farwell settled in Clearwater in 1854, and had an interest in the townsite, but in 1856 came to Maine Prairie and took a claim on the southwest side of Cornelian lake. He built a house and large barn Mr Farwell took an active and leading part in town affairs and was elected to several town offices. He was born in Compton, Canada.

DUDLEY S FRENCH.

Among the first to arrive on the Prairie and settle was Dudley S. French. He came from New York, where he was born and raised. His wife and five children, Herbert M., Francis M., Helen, Amanda, and Harriett, soon joined him. There was no doctor on the Prairie, and as he had studied medicine, he began to practice Homeopathy, and for a number of years was the only physician in the town.

DAVID FOWLER.

David W. Fowler was born in New

Brunswick, in 1825. He came to Maine Prairie in 1856, and took a claim. In 1862 he was married and built the house that he has occupied ever since. He has held town offices, and has been one of the school board for many years. He was one of the sergeants of the home guards during the Indian outbreak in 1862, while the fort was occupied.

JOHN H. FRENCH.

John Hiro French was born in the town of Wheeler, New York, in 1828. He was one of the first to locate on Maine Prairie, in 1856. He assisted in building the first house, and in breaking the first land, and drove the first team through from Little Prairie to Maine Prairie. He had, the year previous, bought a claim near Minneapolis, but sold it soon after. The first claim he took on the Prairie was "jumped" and he took another one. Mr. French has held the office of Supervisor four years, and was clerk of his School Board eight years. For may years he represented the Republican party in county and district conventions. His sisters, Almira and Marilla settled on the Prairie in 1856. Both took and operated claims a number of years.

JOHN P. GUPTILL.

John P. Guptill was one of the early settlers, coming from Maine in 1856. His wife and daughters Margaret, Mary and Emma, and his sons A.D., Albert, Gilbert and Willbert joined him the next year. He enlisted in the 4th Minnesota Regiment and died in a Southern hospital. His son A. D , has carried on the homestead and kept store since he was old enough. He was a member of the school board for several years. Albert Guptill enlisted in the 4th Minnesota Regiment and served about one year and was discharged. He re-enlisted in 1864, in the 2d Minnesota Cavalry, and went out on the frontier as patrol guard and served one year. He was in several battles.

WILLIAM HEYWOOD.

William Heywood came from Albion, Maine, in 1856, accompanied by his two sons William L. and Milton. Mr. Heywood was one of the collectors chosen in early times. He also held other important town offices. But in a few years was called to a better land, and peacefully passed over the dark river. His son, Wm. L. Heywood, continued to operate the farm his father had taken. He was born in Maine in 1832. He takes a deep interest in town and school affairs, and has held the office of town supervisor and school clerk many years. His brother Milton moved to Minneapolis many years ago.

JAMES M. KIMBALL.

James M. Kimball was born in Summersett county, Maine, in 1825. In 1846 he moved to Wisconsin and engaged in the lumber business. He came to and settled in that part of Maine Prairie called Kimball Prairie, in July, 1856, and took up the claim that he has resided on ever since. He married Miss Margaret Dolan. Mr. Kimball has been a successful farmer, attending strictly to his business, and operating his farm in an intelligent manner. His brother-in-law,

JOHN C. DOLAN,

was born in Ireland, in 1831. He lived in New Hampshire five years, and also some time in Illinois, and arrived in Kimball Prairie in 1858. He was a single man. He was an intelligent and successful farmer, owning a farm of 400 acres.

F. M. KIMBALL.

Fry M. Kimball was born in Massachusetts in 1824, and arrived at Maine Prairie in 1856, with his wife and son Gilbert and daughter Nellie. He took a claim and operated it until 1884, when he moved to Minneapolis. He had followed the trade of paper maker until he came to Minnesota He was elected one of the first constables at the time Maine Prairie was organized as a separate town.

EDWIN KIDDER.

Edwin Kidder was born in Maine in 1829, and took a claim on the Prairie in 1856. He enlisted in the 4th Minnesota Regiment in 1861, and served three years.

He was in many of the fiercest battles of the war. Returning to Maine Prairie, he cultivated his farm for many years. He held prominent town offices nearly all of the time, and was a leading member of the Patrons of Husbandry.

A. F. PERKINS.

A F. Perkins was born in Enfield, Maine, in 1833, and came to Maine Prairie in 1856. He took a claim, built a house and improved his farm until 1861, when he enlisted in the 1st Minnesota Regiment, and after serving one year was transferred to the 1st United States Cavalry. He was in many of the principal engagements of the war, being engaged in forty-two battles and skirmishes. He served three years and two months. In August, 1864, he was wounded, and in January, 1865 was discharged. Returning home he was married that spring. After operating his farm for 21 years he moved to St. Cloud. He was justice of the Peace six years, and held other town and school offices and was a prominent member of the Lyceum and Grange.

DANIEL F. PERKINS.

Daniel F. Perkins was born in Maine in 1829, and arrived and took up a claim in Maine Prairie in 1856. He enlisted in the 4th Regiment in 1861. In 1863, while charging on the works at Vicksburg he was killed.

DANIEL SPAULDING.

One of the old and prominent early settlers of Maine Prairie was Daniel Spaulding. He was born in Kennebec county, Maine, in 1813, and came to Maine Prairie in 1856. His wife and sons, Alonso, David, Thomas and George, joined him in the fall; He took a claim and lived on it until his death, in 1886. His wife survived him three years. Mr. Spaulding was deacon of the Methodist church and was the mainstay of that church while he lived.

GEORGE SPAULDING.

Geo. Spaulding was born in Maine in 1844. He enlisted with his brother in the Mounted Rangers and served in General Sibley's expedition against the Sioux Indians in 1862. Since then he bought his present farm, and has carried it on for many years.

THOMAS STRAW.

In 1856, Thomas Straw bought out Wm. Milligan's claim, on Kimball Prairie, and farmed it until 1861, when he enlisted in the 4th Regiment. After the war he returned to his farm and carried it on until his death.

MICHAEL L. PATTEN.

Michael L. Patten was born in Cherryfield, Maine, in 1805. He made several trips to California, when they had to go by team. He arrived in Kimball Prairie in 1858, and took a claim. While in Maine, he was called out as a soldier to guard the northern boundary line against an invasion from Canada. He was postmaster three years from 1867. He spent seven years in California, engaged in lumbering and mining. Mrs. Patten was the first white woman in that part of the town. They kept a hotel for many years.

A. WADE.

A. Wade came to Maine Prairie, in 1856, and took a claim. He was born in Waterville, Maine, in 1833. In 1861 he enlisted in the 4th Regiment. After serving one year he was discharged for disability. He was married in 1872. He cultivated his farm until 1892, when he moved near Kimball. He persistently refused to serve in any official capacity, preferring a quiet life at home.

SAMUEL YOUNG.

Samuel Young was born in Newport, Maine, in 1825. He came to Maine Prairie in 1856, and took a claim and has farmed it ever since He married Miss French, October, 1861. He was elected one of the first supervisors of Fair Haven, and was on the Board three years in Maine Prairie and has also been a member of the School Board. He has been an intelligent and successfull farmer.

JOSEPH E YOUNG.

His brother, Joseph E Young, was born in Newport, Maine, in 1831, and arrived in Maine Prairie, in 1856, and took a claim and farmed it until he died in 1870.

D. A. HOYT.

In the summer of 1856, D. A. Hoyt arrived in Maine Prairie and located a claim. He was born in Aroostic county, Maine, in 1829. He was a farmer. He tiled his farm and built a house, and in 1859, he married the widow of Geo. R. Whitney, of Fair Haven. The result of this marriage was two sons, Charles W. and F. A. Hoyt. In 1867, Mr. Hoyt moved into St. Cloud and went into the woods, to lumber and returned to his farm, in 1869, and farmed it until 1884, when he again moved into St. Cloud and engaged in the real estate business. He died in 1893. His son, Charles W. Hoyt, studied law and is now located at Duluth. The other son, F. A. Hoyt, studied dentistry and is now practicing in St. Cloud.

A. S GREELY.

A. S. Greely was born in Palermo, Maine, in 1830, came to Maine Prairie in 1856, and located on a farm. In connection with his cousin, A. B. Greely, he operated the first reaping machine, and threshing machine, that was run on the Prairie. He married Miss Eliza Clark in 1860. They had three sons and a daughter, George, Jacob and Alvin, and Nellie.

N. I. GREELY.

N. I. Greely was born in Palermo, Maine, in 1833, and arrived in Maine Prairie in 1857, and took a claim adjoining his brother which he operated until his death, in 1892. He was married to Miss Mary Wackley in 1866. They had one son, Albert, and three daughters, Elizabeth, Emma and Alice.

S F. BROWN.

S. F. Brown was born in Massachusetts in 1817, but removed to Rhode Island. From there he came to Maine Prairie in 1857, and took a claim, built a house and began farming. He was the first town clerk of the town, after it was organized as a separate town. He was also elected superintendent of common schools. In 1861, he enlisted in the 4th regiment and rose from the ranks to First Lieutenant in command. At the battle of Vicksburg he was wounded, and while in hospital was delegated on court martial in civil and military commission for three months, until the close of the war. He began studying and practicing medicine in the army, and has continued to practice homeopathy since his return. He has had a large practice.

D. A. ROBERTS.

D. A. Roberts was born in Lyman, Maine, in 1830, and arrived in Maine Prairie in 1857, with his wife and one son, J. O. He took a claim on the east side of Cornelian Lake, and built a house. Afterwards, in 1861, he built a house on the townsite of Marysville, where he resided until 1888, when he moved to Minneapolis. He took an active interest in school matters, and was a member of the school board.

ALEXANDER SPAULDING.

Alexander Spaulding was born in Aroostic county, Maine, in 1839, and came to Maine Prairie in 1857, accompanied by his wife and daughter, Cordelia. He served the town as assessor for nine years. He was the first Postmaster, after the name had been changed, in 1861, to Maine Prairie, and held that office until 1865. He was orderly sergeant of the home guards in 1861. He was one of the enumerators that took the census of the town in the years 1870 and 1875. In connection with operating his farm, he has been engaged in carpentering and house-building.

DAVID SPAULDING.

David Spaulding was Postmaster from 1865 to 1867. He enlisted in the 4th regiment, and remained until the close of the war. After several years he moved to Colorado.

WILLARD SPAULDING.

Willard Spaulding was born in Maine, in 1833. He arrived in the town in 1857, but returned to Maine in 1858, where he was married, and in 1862 returned and bought a farm, on which he has remained

ever since. He has been a member of the town board and also school board of trustees for many years.

THOMAS O. SPAULDING.

Thos. O. Spaulding was born in Smyrna, Maine, in 1838. In 1862 he enlisted in a company of the mounted rangers, and served in the expedition with General Sibley when driving the Sioux Indians back from our state, serving one year. Returning home he bought a farm and has operated it ever since.

ROGER W. STANLEY.

R. W. Stanley was born in Ohio in 1853. He has been engaged in the commercial business on Maine Prairie for a number of years. He attended the Curtis Commercial College in Minneapolis. He has filled the office of Town Treasurer for a number of years.

DAVID B. STANLEY.

David B. Stanley accompanied his parents to Maine Prairie in 1858. He was born in Ohio in 1845. In 1868 he was appointed postmaster, and has held that position ever since, with the exception of two years, when Hoyt & Whitney had it. He has been town clerk for nineteen years, and in 1890 was one of the enumerators and took the census of the town. He has been one of the school board for many years, and in 1878 represented his district in the legislature. In 1868 he was married. He has occupied the same house ever since 1868. He has been engaged in the mercantile business and is a registered pharmacist and dentist. He is a graduate of Bryant & Stratton commercial school, St. Paul, and a notary public.

HENRY WEIDERT.

Among the few Germans who settled in Maine Prairie in the fifties, was Henry Weidert, who was born in Luxemburg, in 1810. In 1857, he came to Maine Prairie, accompanied by his wife and sons, Peter and John, and daughters, Susan, Mary and Marry Ann. Mary Ann died in 1881, Peter is living on his farm in Maine Prairie, John is farming in Benton county. One of his daughters married Mr.

Pent and one married N. Streitz, of St. Cloud town.

ALPHEUS MASERVEY.

Alpheus Maservey was born in the town of Swanton, Vermont, in 1818. At the age of 18, he went to New York, where he remained five years. In 1841, he went to Illinois, and located near Plainfield. In Illinois he engaged in different occupations and spent a year or so operating a sawmill in Missouri. He came to Minnesota at a very early day, located near Dayton, and was one of the very early settlers in St. Cloud. In 1858 he located on a claim in Maine Prairie, where he remained until his death. He was chairman of the board of supervisors and justice of the peace for many years. He was married in Illinois.

JOHN WHITE.

John White was born in Ireland in 1826, and came to America in 1848. He was employed several years in Rhode Island as a clerk in a store. He came to St. Cloud in 1858, and that spring married Miss Margaret Gorman. In the fall they moved on to Maine Prairie and took a homestead. The next spring he moved onto their homestead and has resided there ever since.

CORRECTION.

In the biographical sketch of Wm. Heywood, a mistake was made wherein it was stated: "His son, Wm. L. Heywood, continued to operate the farm his father had taken." The fact is that Wm. Heywood, the father, did not take a claim, but William L., the son, took the claim before his father's arrival on the Prairie, and has operated his claim ever since.

E. H. ATWOOD.

E. H. Atwood was born in Lockport, N. Y., in 1829. He attended school at the Academic Institution at Wilson, N. Y., and taught school one term at Lockport, N. Y. In 1853 he went to Illinois and bought a farm near Springfield. He was married to Miss Augusta Allen, of Gualt, Canada, in 1856. While in Illinois he taught school winters and carried on

his farm in the summer. In 1860 he moved to Maine Prairie with his wife and son, Clarence L. He bought a farm on the south shore of Pearl Lake, and carried it on until 1887, when he rented it and moved into St. Cloud. He was a breeder of full blooded Poland China swine and short-horned cattle. He was an active member of the Grange and Lyceum, and was President of the State Farmers' Alliance in 1888. He was town clerk of his town for many years, and also held the offices at different times of superintendent of schools for the town, assessor and supervisor for several years.

SAMUEL COSSAIRT.

Among the late arrivals was Samuel Cossairt, who bought the John Farwell farm in 1863. He was born in Illinois, in 1815. His family consisted of Henry, Mary, Sarah, Jane, Eliza, Jerry, William and Frank. He operated his farm until his death in 1886. His son John was born in Vermillion county, in 1840, and arrived in Maine Prairie in 1861. In 1866, he moved to Paynesville, but returned to the town again in 1887, where he still resides.

JOSEPH EATON.

Joseph Eaton was born in New Hampshire in 1815 and arrived in Maine Prairie in 1858, with his wife and three children, Lydia, Oren and Mary. He died in 1887. His wife and daughter Mary are in Washington. His son Elmer bought the old homestead and still retains it. He was one of the officers during the Indian troubles in 1862.

MICHAEL GOODNER.

Among the later arrivals in the town were Michael Goodner, with his wife and his sons, David and Henry, and daughters Nancy and Ellen. Mr. Goodner was born in Kentucky in 1807, living awhile in Indiana and Illinois and locating on Maine Prairie in 1862, on a farm which he had bought in 1859. He was a member of the Disiple Church.

DAVID GOODNER.

His son David was born in Illinois in

1844. In 1865 he enlisted in Co. E of the 1st Minnesota heavy artillery, and remained until the close of the war, when he bought a farm and followed that occupation since. Jacob Goodner settled in Maine Prairie in 1862, on section eight. He moved to Kansas in 1877.

WHEELER FRENCH.

Among the later arrivals from New York, were Wheeler French with his wife, an adopted daughter and son, E. J , also his married son, Almon, with his wife and two sons, Wheeler and Luellen. They took claims and carried them on until the death of Wheeler French. Mr. French took great interest in town affairs and was elected to several responsible town offices. His son Almon, together with his sons, operated the home farm for many years. Mr. French was born in Otsego county New York, in 1805.

PERER MORRY.

Peter Morry was born in England in 1821, came to St. Paul in 1858, and to Maine Prairie in 1860, and took his present claim, where he has remained ever since. His wife and daughter Annie, came with him. His son B rt, graduated in an Iowa medical college and is now practicing medicine in Utah.

CHARLES NEAL

In 1859, Charles Neal arrived in Maine Prairie, from Steele county, where he had resided two years. He was born in China, Maine, in 1830. He bought 160 acres of land, and rented it until his return from the war in 1864. He enlisted in the 4th Regiment in 1861 and served three years and was in several severe battles. He was always on duty and never was in a hospital and never had a furlough. He was interested in school matters and was a member of the School Board.

TRUMAN L. STICKNEY.

Among the late arrivals who have been prominent in the affairs of the town and school, T. L. Stickney may be mentioned. He was a native of Erie county, N. Y., having been born there in 1824. In 1870, he arrived in Maine Prairie with his wife

and four children, Frank, S. G., John and daughter Anna, and settled on the farm he has since occupied. He has been instrumental in improving the cattle in his part of the town by keeping fine bred short horns, and inducing his neighbors to improve their stock. He has held the office of supervisor 11 years, and has been a member of the District School Board for fifteen years. He took a leading part in the Patrons of Husbandry.

B. H. WINSLOW.

B. H Winslow was born in Freedom, Maine, in 1834. Came to Fair Haven in 1858, and to Maine Prairie in 1859, and with his family, consisting of wife and one daughter, Ann S., settled on his present farm. He has taken an active interest in town and school affairs and held the office of supervisor eleven years, and also served on the School Board. He took a prominent part in the Patrons of Husbandry, and in the Lyceum. He has raised large flocks of sheep and many cattle.

His brother, J. C. Winslow, was born in 1836, in Freedom, Maine, and enlisted in the 4th Regiment, in 1861, and served three years. In 1872 he moved west. He first settled in Fair Haven in 1857.

NICHOLAS LOESCH.

Nicholas Loesch was born in Grand Dutchey. in 1829, and came to Superior, Minn. In 1856 he went to Rockville, with his parents. In 1863 he married Miss Annie Mouse and settled in Maine Prairie. Mr. Loesch has been a hard working farmer, and by his industry and intelligent management has made a success in farming.

JOHN SCHAFER.

John Schafer was among the early settlers. He was born in Prussia in 1837, and came to Minneapolis in 1856, and in 1858, came to Maine Prairie and took the claim that he has lived on ever since. His father and mother and his two brothers William and Nicholas, and his sisters, Susan and Lana, accompanied him to his new home. Nicholas located on a claim adjoining John's, and William took a farm near by, but in the town of Rockville. Nicholas moved away many years ago, and William has moved to Cold Spring. Susan married Stephen Ethen and Lana married Peter Ethen. The father and mother remained with John until their deaths. John has made a success of farming and now has a fine farm of 640 acres and expects to enlarge it soon by buying more land.

B. U. WATKINS

Bishop B. U. Watkins was born near Carthage, Ohio, Sept. 14th, 1811, and moved to Maine Prairie in May, 1862, accompanied by his wife and sons, William and Joseph R , and daughters Julia and Ida. When but six years old, he was stricken with total blindness. A year after an operation was performed, which partially restored his sight. Notwithstanding his affliction, he persevered in his studies and was educated at Woodward High School in Cincinnati, and became a proficient scholar in the Greek and Latin languages. In his fourth decade he was invited by the American Bible Union to assist in the translation of the New Testament, but declined to serve. He was among the leading Disciples in that part of Ohio and became their minister, and was afterwards given the title of Bishop by some of his people. At Maine Prairie he organized a Disciple church, and held regular services for many years. His wife died in 1870, and in 1872, he married Mrs. Wood, of Ohio. They moved to Cameron, Mo., where he died March 15th, 1892. He was the author of several books and translations from the original Greek and Latin.

T. J. WILEY.

Among the later arrivals, who were prominent in town affairs, was T. J. Wiley, who was born in Meigs county, Ohio, in 1838. He was brought up on a farm, and in 1857 came to Anoka county with his parents. When of age he engaged in lumbering winters and summers at other work. Mr. Wiley and Miss Orlinda Frost were married in 1862. In 1863, they moved to Maine Prairie and pre-empted a homestead which he improved and carried on in connection with running a steam thresher and sawing lumber winters. In 1880 he move to Fergus Falls, but returned to St. Cloud in 1887, where he still resides.

BENJAMIN BARRETT

Benjamin Barrett was born in Meigs county, Ohio, in 1830. He was brought up on a farm. In 1856 he came to Anoka county, Minnesota. He married Miss Mary H. Wiley and in 1861, they moved to Maine Prairie, and located on a farm which he cultivated until he sold it in 1890, when he moved to Excelsior, Minnesota, where he now resides. It 1862, he enlisted in the 1st regiment of Mounted Rangers and operated on the frontiers against the Indians.

ABRAM SHOEMAKER.

Among the later arrivals on Maine Prairie was Abram Shoemaker, who was born in Columbianna county, Ohio, in 1816, where he spent his youth and worked at the cooper trade, but afterwards became a Millwright. He went to Lake county at the age of 22. When 24 years of age he was married, but in a year or so his wife died. He married for his second wife Miss Achsah Waite, and in 1863 came to Wabasha county, Minnesota. In 1872 he came to Maine Prairie, with his wife, three sons, M. E., C. D. and W. A., and two daughters, Mrs. Mason and Mrs. Huntoon. He was ordained a minister in the Disciple church when 25 years old. He never attended school, but two months, and what education he had was acquired at home or in the shop. While working at the cooper trade he had a book propped open on the bench before him and took every possible opportunity to store his mind with useful knowledge, and became a well informed man upon many subjects. He preached for forty-five years, at the same time operating his farm in an intelligent manner. In 1886, he quietly passed away, gladly welcoming the messenger that was to free him from pain and anguish, with bright anticipations of a blessed hereafter, and mourned by all who knew him.

———

This finishes the history of Maine Prairie, and the biographical sketches of all the early settlers which could be obtained. We wish to thank the citizens of that town for their kindness and assistance in this work. If errors have occurred, (and it would be strange if there had not,) they were unintentional, for the great aim of the writer was to give a true history and each person his just dues.

REPORT OF INDIAN FIGHT CORRECT.

The following letter, from Gus. H. Beaulieu, Deputy U. S. Marshal, will explain itself regarding the Indian fight of 1860:

St Paul, Sept. 29, 1895.
E. H. Atwood, Esb., St. Cloud, Minn.

DEAR SIR: Read your letter of the 17th inst., and also one of a previous date, relative to the Indian fight at Maine Prairie.

I know all the Indians (Chippewas) who were engaged in the fight referred to, but only two or three of them are still alive. I read your account of the fight published in the St. Cloud TIMES to Me-sha-ke-keship, one of the Indians engaged in the fight, and who lives at White Earth, and he said it was substantially correct. When I see him again, I will get all the names of the Chippewa participants of the fight and his version of it.

Yours truly,
GEO. H. BEAULIEU.

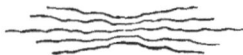

History of Fair Haven.

By E. H. ATWOOD.

FAIR HAVEN THE BEAUTIFUL.

The town of Fair Haven is situated on the south line of Stearns county. It is bordered on the south by the Clearwater river, which is capable of furnishing sufficient water power to run a saw and a flouring mill. The surface of the town is somewhat undulating, and a large part of it, prior to its settlement, was covered with brush and timber. Its soil is very rich and fertile, capable of raising the finest of crops. Extensive marsh meadows abound throughout the town, which produce large quantities of excellent hay, while the timber is valuable for wood, lumber and building material. There are also many beautiful lakes in the town.

The village of Fair Haven is on the extreme south line of the town, and is beautifully located. To the southeast of the village are several beautiful lakes, abounding in the finest kinds of fish. The innumerable bays and indentations around the shores of these lakes; the green sloping banks or wooded sides, make these lakes ideal watering places and summer resorts for those seeking the invigorating atmosphere of Minnesota. The village is beautifully situated on the high banks of the Clearwater river. The deep romantic valley, the rippling murmur of the stream as it courses its way to the lakes below, and on to swell the volume of the Father of waters; the flashing of the sunlight through the trees upon the distant lakes, are scenes that cannot fail to please the eye and inspire the beholder with the grandeur of nature. From elevated points in the village, may be had a splendid view of the surrounding country with its wooded hills, its deep valleys and fertile prairies. The first lake below the village was named Caroline, in honor of Mrs. Thos. C. Partridge. The next is a small one called Mayhew Lake. The next one is named Big Lake, and is two or three miles long. Above the village on the river are three more lakes that are so situated in a secluded valley that they form a fine quiet resort for pleasure seekers. They are called Mariah, Sunda and Lake Mary. Such are the conditions of Fair Haven to-day, but there is no record of any white man having ever been in the territory of the present town of Fair Haven prior to the year 1856. Like Maine Prairie, which town it joins, it was the disputed hunting ground of the Sioux and Chippewa Indians, and the many relics that are found in the vicinity, such as human bones, Indian weapons and rude fortifications, indicate that many sanguinary conflicts between hostile tribes of Indians has transpired in this region.

FIRST DISCOVERY OF FAIR HAVEN.

Thomas C. Partridge has been termed

the Father of Fair Haven. He came from Ohio to Minnesota in the fall of 1854, and built a house in Minneapolis. The next spring he bought a farm nine miles northwest of that city and raised large crops of wheat and oats. In the spring of 1856 he was joined by the following named persons from Ohio: Lovinus Abell, Sylvester Woolcutt, Geo. W. Root, Henry Root, H. Hill, J. G. Smith and John L. Dean. Rumors had reached them of the fertile and well matured region to the west of Clearwater. His party with a team went up the west bank of the Mississippi to discover this locality, and, if found desirable, would locate there and send for their families and establish a colony of eastern people. Many obstacles and difficulties were encountered on their journey, for the roads were poor, with no bridges over the small streams emptying into the Mississippi from the west. When they arrived at Clearwater they made inquiries of the inhabitants concerning the country to the west, and up the Clearwater River, which empties into the Mississippi at that place, but could learn nothing definite regarding the country to the west. They concluded to explore for themselves, and started west up the Clearwater river. It was slow, tedious traveling, and at night they had made but seven miles on their journey, when they went into camp.

TAKING THEIR CLAIMS.

The next morning Partridge, Root and Woolcutt, took several days' rations and, leaving the others in camp, started west on foot. They soon came out on what is now the Fair Haven prairie, and soon after discovered the river, where the present mill is situated. They then located the present mill site. This was on the 27th day of May. The rest of the party was sent for, and came through the same day. They were all delighted with the locality. The green prairie, the fine wooded banks of river and lakes, the clear bracing atmosphere, so pleased them that they impatiently awaited the coming of daylight the next morning that they

might locate their claims. Before night of May 28th they had all staked out their claims near the present village. Mr. Partridge located the town site of Fair Haven, and in July Mr. E. O. Haven was employed to survey and plat the townsite. Henry Root built the first house on his claim near the village during the summer. His house was used as a hotel or stopping place, where new arrivals could remain until they could build a house for themselves. Sometimes, it is claimed, that 20 to 30 persons slept in it at night. The men were busy that summer getting supplies from St. Anthony of food and building material and in clearing and breaking their land.

NEW ARRIVALS.

Some returned to the East after their families, but there were no new arrivals until fall. In October, the following persons were among those that arrived in the new settlement. Aaron Scribner and wife, Wm. H. Day and wife, Mrs. Lovinus Abell and family, consisting of Jane, Newton, Westley, John, Laurie and Milton; Alonson Smith, wife and son Wallace and daughter Mary, and E. G. Parsons. In November, Mrs. T. C. Partridge came with her sons, Payson, Cecil, Florus and daughter Valona. Mrs. Sylvester Woolcutt and two children also arrived, and Joshua Kent and family and Steven C. Kent and wife arrived in June. Still later that fall Mr. V. W. Olds arrived. Mrs. W. H. Day, one of the above party, was ambitious to be the first white woman in Fair Haven, and when within six or seven miles of that place she hastened forward, on foot, ahead of the rest of the party, hoping to be the first to arrive; but when near the end of her journey, she was attracted into the brush to pick some berries. While thus engaged, Mrs. Aaron Scribner, who also had a desire to be the first to reach the place, passed Mrs. Day, and has the satisfaction of being the *first white woman in the village of Fair Haven.* When Mrs. Day arrived she was surprised and chagrined to find Mrs. Scribner on the ground before her. When this party arrived, there was but one house finished and one partly finished, in the town. The newcomers to the number of twenty or thirty, slept in Mr. Root's house the first night.

TOLD IN AN ADDRESS.

The following extract from an address, delivered at a picnic at Long lake by a Fair Havenite, pertains to the discovery of the township:

"And there came a company of men from the Buckeye State, even Ohio, and they looked for a water power. And when they saw the mills at Clearwater they said peradventure we can find a mill site if we follow up the Clearwater river. So they followed it for the space of ten Sabbath days' journey, and found what they sought; and builded a mill. And the place was fair to behold, and was a haven of rest for the weary. Now, therefore, called they it Fair Haven. And there was Thomas the Partridge, and Sylvester whose surname was Woolcutt, and Lovinus t' e Abell, and Alanson the Smith, and many young men. And they builded an house and dwelt therein at night, but in the day they worked on their claims And it came to pass, that they had no lumber to build the stairs to the house. So they made a ladder of sticks, wherewith to climb to the loft to sleep. And the roof was low, so that no man could stand under it, and it was so that the first one in the loft laid down and rolled under the roof and the next one rolled against him and so on till all were in the loft, and they filled it full, so that no man could turn over without the rest turned over also for they lay spoon fashion. And they cut logs and built houses each man for himself, and when they had made an end of building they brought their wives and children and each lived in his own house. And many others came to Fair Haven and dwelt there. James the Tucker, and John the Noyesy Man, Albertis the carpenter, George the clever, and Uncle John his brother. And they were sore distressed for bread, for the mill

was not yet finished to grind their corn. But one, Charles, who is called Dally, had a mill to grind corn and they called it a "coffee mill" in derision, for it was small. When the people had not meal they pounded their corn in a morter, and mixed it with water, baking it in pans and made cakes of it. The cakes called they bannocks. And they murmered because they had to pound their corn and were glad to go to the "coffee mill" though it was small. And they caught many fish, even suckers, and their food was bannock and dried suckers. Then Ambrose W., son of James the Tucker, took a boat and went in search of the little mill, for it grieved him to pound corn, and he found the mill and got his meal, and when he had made an end of his journeyings he told the people of Fair Haven that he had discovered some other settlers, who had come from the great city, the city of churches; and that they had settled on the banks of Clearwater Lake, and dwelt there, and the land was exceedingly rich and they tilled the land and raised wheat and cattle and horses And the lake swarmed with fine fish, and they caught fish and cooked and gave to Ambrose, and he did eat. And the name of the head of the family was Octavius, and they had many sons and daughters. And they were worthy people and of mighty stature, therefore they were called Longworths. And when Ambrose had made an end of speaking, the people cried out with one accord and said: 'Let us go and see the Longworths, and have a good time.' And many people gathered there from that day forth, and picnics, and sociables, and harvest home festivals, and tea parties, were held there, for they said: 'Do we not always have a good time? Yea verily.' Now the rest of these chronicles how Fair Haven built up and new families came in and old ones died out, and moved away. Are they not written in the memories of the people?"

BRAVERY OF PIONEER WOMEN.

An incident occurred in the fall of 1856 that showed the bravery of these pioneer women. Mr. Stephen C. Kent had taken a claim four miles from the village and built a house and began housekeeping. There were but one or two other houses within several miles. Mr. Kent was compelled to be absent at times. A large band of Indians were camped not far off, and during the day time the house would be visited by many of these hunters. These Indians were hunting deer and in three weeks had killed seven hundred. One day quite a number of them had gathered in and around the house. A huge Indian chief was inside the house and saw some powder and shot on a shelf and asked Mrs. Kent for them, but she told him he could not have them. The Indian paid no attention to her reply but started to get the ammunition. Quick as a flash Mrs. Kent seized a loaded gun and took a deadly aim at the Indian. The savage was taken by surprise, and badly frightened. He wheeled and sprang through the door and never stopped until out of range of the deadly gun. The other Indians laughed and hooted at the discomfited warrior fleeing from a white squaw, and then turned to Mrs. Kent and shouted: "White squaw brave," "brave white squaw," and seemed to greatly admire the plucky white "squaw." The Indians after this test of her bravery, never molested her and seemed to have a great respect for her.

BUSY WINTER FOR SETTLERS

The winter of 1856-7 was a busy one for the pioneers. Houses and stables had to be built; supplies of provisions and goods had to be hauled from St. Anthony Material for the saw mill and dam was hauled out of the timber by a crew of men. T. C. Partridge, a Free Baptist, conducted religious meetings in his big log house, and members of other denominations joined in the exercises, and nothing was said about sect. These pioneers were an educated and intelligent class of people, and had come from localities where they had access to scientific and literary lectures and magazines, and societies for the moral, social, and intellectual development of its mem-

bers. In their new home with poor mail facilities, and their distance from large cities they were deprived of many of their old time enjoyments, and were consequently thrown upon their own resources to discover something to take the place of their lost intellectual pleasures. Soon

A LITERARY SOCIETY

was started, and two papers were very ably edited by the members. One was managed by the lady members, and the other by the male members, and read at their meetings alternately, followed by debates, declamations, dialogues and music. This society was kept up for many years In 1859, they permanently organized their society by adopting a constitution and by-laws. The following is an account of this meeting taken from the secretary's book:

"FAIR HAVEN, Nov. 24, 1859.

"Fair Haven Literary Association met and organized by appointing officers as follows: President, J. C. Boobar; Vice President, V. W. Olds; Secretary, J W. Coats; Treasurer, James Jenks; Committee, Ambrose Tucker; Editor of *Knapsack*, A. Montgomery.

"The foregoing constitution and by-laws were also adopted at this meeting and Miss E. Tucker was appointed Editress of the Ladies' *Budget*. J. W. Coats, secretary.

"Names of members of Fair Haven Literary Society:

"J. C. Boobar, V. W. Olds, B. F. Butler, J. O. Rice, A. W. Tucker, S. Woolcutt, J. L. Dean, J. G. Smith, P. C. Townsend, G. W. Townsend, W. C. Tuft, John Dean, N. M. Scovill, James Jenks, D. Spaulding, D. A. Perkins, A. Montgomery, Wm. Rice, T. C. Partridge, A. M. Durand, C. A. Robinson, J. W. Coats, J. C. Winslow, N. Abell."

This society had many members of superior intellectual attainments, and their meetings were social and literary events, seldom equaled in any community. Music of a superior order was furnished by its members, as well as original essays that were interesting and possessed of much intrinsic worth. The old settlers look back with pride to the many meritorious literary production that were read at their meetings, and their eyes kindle with enthusiasm when they speak of their "feasts of reason," and they wonder why it is that the rising generation with all the advantages for education and learning do not seem to enjoy such literary entertainments.

A DEBATING SOCIETY.

The following account of the organization of a young men's debating soci-ty is taken from the secretary's record book. There was also a long constitution and by-laws and set of rules governing their deportment while debating:

"FAIR HAVEN, Oct. 15, 1859.

The young men of Fair Haven met pursuant to call, for the purpose of considering the propriety of organizing a debating club, the object of which should be the intellectual and social development of its members. The preliminary organization was effected by appointing A. W. Tucker, president; V. W. Olds, secretary.

B. F. Butler presented a constitution and by-laws for the consideration of the meeting which were unanimously adopted. The club then proceeded to elect officers for the ensuing week. J. L. Dean was chosen president, D. A. Perkins vice president, A. W. Tucker secretary V. W. Olds treasurer, P. P. Partridge marshal.

Names of the members of the young men's debating club: A. W. Tucker, B. F. Butler, C. A. Robinson, V. W. Olds, J. C. Winslow, N. Abell, D. A. Perkins, T. J. Woodworth, T. J. R binson, Benj. Plummer, G. W. Dean, J. L. Dean, C. W. West."

The club was kept up for some time, but many of its most active members joined the army to assist in puttting down the rebellion in 1861, and the club ceased to exist.

MRS. SWISSHELM AND STEPHEN MILLER.

The following account was given the writer by one of the active members of the Fair Haven Literary Society, who was there and saw and felt the things whereof he speaks:

"There was one thing connected with this Lyceum that may perhaps deserve more than a passing notice and may be of extra interest to St. Cloud readers. James Jenks was appointed a committee of one to hunt up something new for the edification of the society. This was during the winter of 1858-9. There had been two years of grasshoppers; there was no old grain; everybody was speculating in town lots; wolves and bears were the occupants of most paper cities; Mrs. Jane G. Swisshelm's printing outfit had been thrown into the Mississippi, just below where the Normal School now stands; a solemn compact had been entered into, that the St. Cloud Visitor, (Mrs. Swisshelm's paper,) should never again allude to the destruction of its office, and she had completely turned the tables upon her persecutors. (Those are her own words.) Mr. Jenks was able to grasp the situation and thought that a lecture from Mrs. Swisshelm would be a drawing card. He succeeded in persuading that lady to go out to Fair Haven and lecture before the Lyceum. Stephen Miller, a relative of her husband, and afterwards Governor of Minnesota, drove the team that took the famous controversialist to Fair Haven. Standing room was at a premium in the little slab shanty that served for a lecture room. As there seemed to be no other place for them to go, Mr. Jenks took them home with him. His house consisted of one low room fifteen by twenty-four feet. A quilt partition strung across the room ten feet from the rear end to make a double bed room. Mrs. Jenks gave up her bed to Mrs. Swisshelm and with her baby shared a cot with Mary Abby (now Mrs. W. H. Thompson, of St. Cloud,) while the future Governor Miller slept on the floor with Mr. Jenks, rolled up in buffalo robes, with their feet to the cook stove, where a rousing fire was kept all night. In after life Mrs. Swisshelm is said to have declared that she never slept

more comfortably, although there was but
one inch of basswood between her bed and
40 degrees below zero; although she could
see the stars through the cracks in the
roof, and although the wolves howled in
the public square only 66 feet away. It
was on this occasion that Fair Haven discovered that Stephen Miller was the best
stump speaker in the State.

ARRIVALS IN 1857.

The winter of 1856-7 had passed, and the
farmers began clearing, plowing, sowing
and planting, while at the same time a
crew of men and teams were busy hauling
material for the dam and saw mill and
erecting the mill and building the dam
across the Clearwater river. In April a
large party from Ohio arrived and joined
the new settlement; most of them took
claims near the village. Among this party
were J. W. Coats, A. J. Brockett, Miner
Sperry, Newton Scovill, Charles Abell,
Lucius Belden, Alfred Dean and wife,
Geo. W. Dean, wife and children, A.
Montgomery and wife, Mrs. Alanson
Smith and son, Wallace, and daughters,
Elvira and Mary. The arrivals in May
were John K. Noyes and wife and chil-
dren, Josephine, Lizzie, Mary, Bernice,
George, Laura, Julia and Frank. During
the summer the arrivals in the new settle-
ment were J. C. Winslow, D. A. Perkins,
Josiah Noyes, A. J. Whitney, Joseph H.
Lock, wife and family, James Tucker,
with wife and children, Sarah, Ambrose,
Eliza, Georgianna and Nellie; Eligah
Townsend, with wife and sons, Perry, Geo.
W., Erwin, Jason, Leonard and daughters,
Sarah Ann and Almira.

FIRST DEATH—FIRST MARRIAGE.

About the only event that occurred to
mar the happiness of the pioneers this
spring in their new home was the death
of Theron Dean, son of Geo. W. Dean,
whose death was caused by an attack of
measles. The family had arrived that
spring from Ohio, and this loss was keenly
felt by the entire community. This was
the first death in the new settlement.
Henry Root and Miss Aurilla Dean were

joined in the holy bonds of matrimony
this year, being the first marriage in Fair
Haven, according to the authority of Elder
Partridge, who performed the ceremony.
The village was growing and many new
houses were being erected.

MERCANTILE VENTURES.

Charles Abell put in a general stock of
merchandise during the summer and
opened a store. In the fall T. C. Partridge
and Hazzard started a clothing store; and
J. K. Noyes erected a large log building,
which he used as a hotel until he finished
his large Octagon hotel.

FINANCIAL DEPRESSION—GRASSHOPPERS.

The year of 1857 will long be remembered as the year of the great financial
crash that prostrated the business of the
country and ruined so many people. The
pioneers keenly felt the depression, and to
add to their hardships, the grasshoppers
made their appearance, just as their fields
were golden with ripened wheat and oats.
Strenuous efforts were made to protect the
grain, but in vain. They were forced to
stand and see the fruit of their summer's
labor, the crop on which so much toil had
been expended and on which was centered
all their hopes of sustenance during the
rigor of a Minnesota winter, consumed by
those insatiable insects, that stopped not
when the fields were ravished and laid
bare, but then attacked the gardens. The
hungry swarm devoured all the vegetables,
saving a few a patches here and there that
were partially saved.

DISTRESSING SITUATION.

The situation of the pioneers, with their
winter's supply of food destroyed, and none
to be had this side of St. Anthony, 65
miles away, was indeed a distressing one.
Add to this the fact that corn cost the ex-
horbitant sum of two dollars per bushel,
and the settlers had little or no money to
buy with, having nearly exhausted their
means in improving their homes and purchasing supplies of food and clothing and
other necessaries, and the situation as-
sumes an aspect calculated to make the
stoutest heart quail. But these early

pioneers of Fair Haven were not so easily discouraged. They were full of hope for the future, and began to prepare for the coming winter with undaunted courage. The few bushels of poor wheat were taken in a boat to a small mill at the foot of the lake, where it was converted into cracked wheat. In order to eke out the scanty supply of corn and potatoes that they were able to procure, large quantities of fish were caught in the neighboring lakes and streams, and were salted and dried. At certain times of the year, when the fish were running up the streams to spawn, wagon loads of suckers could be caught in a single night. These fish are excellent when caught in the early spring. Besides suckers there were large quantities of pike, pickerel, bass, sunfish and other kinds found in the lakes and streams near the village. As there were plenty of deer, bear and other wild animals, their meat was used as food. In Fair Haven, as well as in the town of Maine Prairie, the old inhabitants say that wheat flour was a luxury that but few, if any, could indulge in that winter. In Maine Prairie, it is learned from a reliable source, that but one family had any wheat flour in the house that winter, and this family had only a pail full, which they kept all winter, just to say that they were not out of flour. Many families were reduced to live on potatoes and salt or corn meal, at times being unable to procure both articles of food at the same time. But, notwithstanding their privations, these people were healthy, hearty and jolly, and in conversation with them now, they enjoy telling of their privations and the many schemes used to get a little corn meal, or a few potatoes and salt. Sugar, tea, coffee and store tobacco were luxuries that but few could indulge in.

An amusing story is told of a widow with a large family of children, who found that her last pound of corn meal was gone and the children were hungry and only a few potatoes remained in the cellar. The situation was desperate and something must be done and that quickly. With the skill that great emergencies beget in woman quite as well as in man, this widow rose to the occasion. By a brilliant and unique commercial transaction, the details of which she has never been able to explain, only that it was a fair and honorable deal, she became the possessor of a sack of corn, and hastened her eldest son in a boat with the precious charge off to the little mill at the foot of the lake, to get it ground, so that they could have some corn bread. During his absence the children appeased their hunger with roast potatoes and salt. About the time that the son should be returning and would be upon the lake, a terrible storm arose, and it was feared that the boat would be swamped and the boy drowned. Extreme pangs of hunger seems to deaden the natural affections, for 'tis said that the widow paced her room wringing her hands in great distress and burst forth with the exclamation: "O, dear, what will we do for supper if the boy is drowned and the meal lost." But strong men had gone to the assistance of the lad, and soon had him and the precious corn meal at home in safety, and the children had their fill of Johnny cake.

Early in the spring it was learned that the Legislature had made an appropriation to assist the grasshopper sufferers, and Mr. L. Belden volunteered to go to St. Paul with his ox team and procure aid from this appropriation. He had no money to pay his way, but the people on the way were very hospitable and kept him and his team without pay. When he arrived at Minneapolis he learned that the State appropriation had been exhausted, but when he told his story to the business men of Minneapolis, with their proverbial generosity and public spirit, contributed a quantity of provisions, consisting of eleven barrels of flour, two sacks of beans, a quantity of beef and pork, garden seeds and some other things. Mr. Belden hauled one load with his team and shipped the balance by boat to Clearwater. At that time a steam boat made regular trips from Minneapolis to St. Cloud. When Mr. Belden reached Fair Haven, a team was sent to Clearwater for the provision that come up on the boat. The settlers were overjoyed upon the arrival of the much needed supplies, which were distributed among the more needy ones. These early settlers have always remembered the kindness of the Minneapolis business men and cherish a warm feeling toward that city.

ARRIVALS IN 1858.

The following are among the arrivals this year: Stinson Lovejoy and wife, Frank Crane, John Metcalf, B. H. Winslow and wife and daughter, Ann S., Michael Patten and family, Mrs. Geo. R. Whitney and family, consisting of Mary A., Alberton, Geo. R, Horace and F. H., J. C. Boobar, wife and large family, consisting of Anna M., Druzilla, Lucy, Henry, Althea, Geo. Rosco, Charlotte, Harritt C., Hannah W., James Elmer, James Jenks and wife, O. D. Webb and family, consisting of wife and daughters, Alma, Ella and Emma.

It was a difficult task for the settlers to procure sufficient seed wheat, oats, corn and garden seeds to plant their fields and gardens, this spring, and at the same time keep themselves supplied with food, to sustain them until the new crop came in In order to get these needed supplies, money had to be borrowed for which they were charged from two to five per cent per month interest. This shows that the modern Shylock, who charges ten per cent. interest per annum and two per cent. bonus for loans, is not "in it," when compared with those who throve on the misfortunes of others, 37 years ago. The rich settlers had spent all of their money, and were but little better off than the poor. Supplies of all kinds were scarce and hard to obtain. Corn cost two dollars per bushel with freight added, and other provisions were proportionally dear. Notwithstanding the hard times, short rations, and old clothes, these pioneers were

cheerful and the boys and girls had their fun. There was marrying and giving in marriage, and parties and balls, dancing schools and prayer meetings, followed each other in rapid succession.

FOURTH OF JULY CELEBRATION.

On the Fourth of July, 1858, the Fair Havenites had their first celebration. Tables were set in the public square, where all ate together. Although the times were hard and the bill of fare not elaborate, this particular day is remembered as one of the pleasant epochs of that period. The time was passed with speeches and plenty of music by the Glee Club. J. W. Coats and A. Montgomery composed an original song, with words and tune in perfect harmony, which they sang to the great delight of their audience. It was the event of the day, and a few lines of this song are still hummed by some of the oldest settlers. The song portrayed many of their hardships in a comical manner, and also hit off in a witty and amusing style many of the people and incidents connected with the times.

MARRIAGE AND CHARIVARI.

The following incident is related by a Fair Havenite, who was a young girl at the time, and who distinctly remembers all about it: In July of this year John L. Dean and Sarah Tucker were to be quietly married. Great pains had been taken to guard the secret of the intended ceremony and let only the two families of the contracting parties know of the affair, and it was thought that all their friends were wholly ignorant of the prospective event. It was in the evening after prayer meeting that the minister quietly stepped into Mr. Tucker's house and performed the ceremony that made them man and wife. It was supposed that only those present knew of the wedding. But the small boys of that period were sharp as a modern newspaper reporter. They soon discovered that the window shade of a window opening into the main room of the Tucker house was not quite down, leaving a two inch space where the boys could view the whole ceremony and hear what was said. It is claimed that the boy who first discovered the view of vantage was a fair minded youth, and was not exorbitant in his charges to the other lads for an occasional glimpse at the proceedings through the narrow opening. As soon as the ceremony was over the young men and boys decided to give the couple a grand charivari. As soon as "tired nature's sweet restorer" had claimed each and all the happy participants, and the calm of midnight's holy hour was over all the peaceful settlement, the stillness of the night was sharply and rudely broken by the reports of many guns accompanied by the ringing of bells and the wild whoops and yells of the serenaders

As there had been some uneasiness felt by the citizens on account of some movements of the Indians, the startled inhabitants, when they heard the firing, accompanied by whoops, in which the revelers endeavored to imitate the war whoop of the savages, together with some Indian jargon, thought that surely the Indians had attacked the town and were murdering and torturing the people. The alarm was universal and many fled into the brush, in their haste with only their night clothes on. Others prepared to get into boats and row out into the lake. But the serenaders soon learned that the people were frightened and fleeing. They thereupon hastened to let the facts in the case be known. One badly frightened mother aroused her large family, and although the frightful din was gradually approaching her house, and the children were wild with fear and were anxious to flee into the brush and hide, yet she restrained them for she had been brought up in the east and had been taught that the rules of propriety should be observed under all conditions, and she insisted that the children should have their faces washed and especially her young girl, should have her hair combed and be properly dressed before seeking safety in flight. It is safe to say that this particular wedding will long be remembered.

INDIANS.

Later in the season a large encampment of Sioux hunters with their families pitched their tents about a mile north of the village. They had been very successful in their hunts and had slain large numbers of deer, bear and other game. But one day, without any apparent cause (unless they had seen signs of their deadly foes, the Ch'ppewas') they hastily and in much confusion took down their tents and hurried across the river south-east of the town to a spot near lake Sylvia where they fortified themselves by building breastworks of logs. Soon after this they went off to the south and were seen no more that season.

FIRST POST OFFICE.

A Post office was established this year at Fair Haven and John K. Noyes was appointed postmaster, being the first one in the town.

TOWN ORGANIZED 1859.

"The town of Fair Haven was organized ized this spring as a separate town, and the first town meeting was held pursuant to an order of the Board of County Commissioners, which order stated that said town meeting was to be held April 5, 1859. Accordingly a meeting was called to meet at that time.

MINUTES OF FIRST TOWN MEETING.

At the town meeting held at Fair Haven, April 5, 1859, T. C. Partridge was chosen temporary chairman. The voters then proceeded to elect officers for the day, and Mr. Calvin J. Boobar was chosen moderator, and Albertis Montgomery clerk, and, being sworn into office, Messrs. Samuel Young, M. L. Patten and N. J. Robinson were chosen judges of election. The polls were opened, and the electors then proceeded to vote for officers Voted to adjourn at twelve and meet again at one. At the proper time the moderator declared the polls closed, and the judges proceeded to canvass the votes, and declared the following persons elected: Chairman of Supervisors, Albertis Montgomery; 2d Supervisor, T. C. Partridge; 3d Supervisor, S. Young; Clerk, James Jenks; Assessor, J H. Locke; Collector, Wm. Heywood; Overseer of the Poor, H. H. Mayo; Constables, G. A. Bibber and Sumner Leavitt; Justices of the Peace, H. P. Bennett and C. J. Boobar. J. P. Taylor and John H.K. Noyes were chosen overseers of highways; J. K. Noyes, pound master. The electors then voted to raise a tax of fifty dollars for township purposes. Voted to meet at J P. Taylor's for the next meeting of the town. On motion adjourned.

ALBERTIS MONTGOMERY, Clerk."

Forty-four voted at this meeting.

EVENTS IN 1859.

There were but few arrivals in Fair Haven during 1859, but there was increased activity in the new settlement. The fine water power was capable of running more machinery than one saw mill. O. D. Webb began the erection of a flouring mill. Such a mill was greatly needed, for there was no place near where the farmers could get their wheat ground into flour, and the completion of this mill was hailed with great rejoicing.

Among the arrivals this year was O. S. Senter, a Congregational minister. He married Mrs. Stevenson, a widow, daughter of Mr. and Mrs. Abel Kent. The wife died in about a year and Mr. Senter went to California.

In 1859, there was a large band of Sioux, said to number 100 warriors, with 200 squaws and young Indians, encamped northwest of Fair Haven, hunting game. Deer were very plentiful, and it was said that these Indians killed immense numbers while thus encamped. They were peaceably inclined, still, with that number of Indians so near, and with the knowledge that their friendship did not emanate from the heart, and that in their inmost souls they hated the whites, there was a feeling of uneasiness, especially among the women who had read of the treachery and cruelty of these savages.

The St. Cloud *Democrat* of March 24, 1859, had this Fair Haven item: "School District No. 1 was organized March 14, 1859, by electing C. J. Boobar, A. C. Smith and A. Montgomery trustees and James Jenks District Clerk."

BANNER REPUBLICAN TOWN.

Fair Haven was considered the banner Republican town of Stearns county. The number of Democratic votes usually cast at elections was quite small, and at one general election it is claimed that there was not a Democratic vote cast. There was great rejoicing when it was known that Abraham Lincoln was nominated, and much interest was manifested throughout the campaign. Their feelings reached a high pitch of enthusiasm when he was elected President, and they showed their joy by kindling huge bonfires, and with speeches and songs expressed their happiness at the result of the election.

EVENTS IN 1860.

The condition of the settlers began to improve in many respects. The crops this year were good and there was plenty to eat of such as could be raised in this locality. But the prices that they could obtain for such produce as they had raised was very small. It took about fifteen bushels of wheat to buy a barrel of salt, and such luxuries as sugar, tea, coffee and store tobacco, were left for visitors, only in many homes. Browned peas and barley, as well as browned crusts of bread were used as a substitute for coffee by a large majority of the families. One would naturally suppose that under such conditions of privation the people would be downcast and gloomy. But such was not the case. All looked forward to a bright and glorious future. Hope, the well-spring of life, was largely developed in the hearts of these pioneers. These privations were considered only temporary, and would, in the near future, pass away. In the meanwhile their time was occupied in developing the country and improving their farms. In the winter the literary feasts of their Lyceum were greatly enjoyed, as well as their church festivals, donations and social meetings. Thus passed the winter of 1860-1.

PATRIOTISM IN FAIR HAVEN.

The citizens of Fair Haven did not lack in patriotism, and when the war of the rebellion broke out they propose 1 to do their p rt toward putting it down. They held meetings and discussed the question, and many signified their desire to enlist should the war continue. As soon as the harvest was over, and the President had called for more troops, a number volunteered. The following are among those that enlisted at diff rent times: In the First Minnesota Regiment, Perry C. Townsand, Geo. W. Townsand, R. M. E stman. John Abell, D. A. Perkins, G. Sias and Jerome Baldwin. The latter died Aug. 11th, 1864, at David's Island, New York Harbor. Charles Robinson enlisted in the Second Minnesota Regiment, and Ambrose W. Tucker in the Third. In October, 1861, the following enlisted from Fair Haven: In Company D, Fourth Minnesota Regiment, with Thomas E. Inman as Captain, B. F. Butler, A. J. Whitney, W. C. Tufts, Milo M. Scoville, Thadeus I Robinson, H. Boobar, Ruben Wheeler, Benjamin Plummer, and Newton A. Abell. S. C. and Albert Kemp and Jerome Pratt enlisted in Hatche's Battalion. John B Inman joined the First Regiment of Heavy Artillery in February, 1865.

In 1863, A. Farnsworth, B. F. Butler, A. W. Tucker, James Robinson, L. H. Brown, Elder Norris and John L Dean joined the State's scouts. Of the volunteers of Company D, Fourth Minnesota Regiment, the following met death beneath a strange sky and on unknown soil: Thadeus I. Robinson, at Vicksburg, Mississippi, July 24, 1863; H. C. Boobar, at Clear Cre-k, Miss., Aug. 18, 1862; Milo M. Scoville, at Farmington, Miss, July 5, 1862. With so many young men absent fighting for their country, and exposed to the perils of war in battles and sickness in pestilential southern swamps, the citizens of Fair Haven had little cause for joy and many of their literary and social events were given up. There were many whose thoughts and affections were with the loved ones on southern fields, so that the year 1861 passed without particular incident at home.

SIOUX OUTBREAK OF 1862.

As a large number of the young men of Fair Haven had enlisted for the war and had gone south in the summer and fall of 1861, to fight for their country, there were few if any of the people of that town but had some one near and dear to them in the army. It was either father, brother, sweetheart, relative or friend, and very few if any were indifferent to the results of the mighty conflict that was raging on southern battle fields. Both the northern and southern forces had, during the winter of 1861, made gigantic preparations for the campaign of 1862, and great anxiety was felt for the loved ones that were to engage in the fierce battles so soon to be fought. The spring of 1862 found the citizens of Fair Haven like those in thousands of other hamlets throughout the northern states, in an anxious mood. But, with silent prayers for the safety of the relatives and friends in far away camps, they worked on farms, in shops and in factories, hoping that the war would soon be over and peace again reign. This was their condition in August. Everything was quiet at home, and all were engaged in securing a most bountiful crop of all kinds of grain and other farm produce, when, like a thunderbolt from a clear sky, the news came of the massacre of the whites and the battle between the Sioux Indians and the soldiers on the Minnesota river. For a short time this news occasioned much excitement and confusion. Very soon large numbers of refugees who had been driven from their peaceful homes on the frontier beyond the Big Woods, fleeing for their lives, began passing through the village on their way to a place of safety, bringing with them daily and hourly, additional tal-s of the fiendish cruelties and horrible atrocities perpetrated upon the

helpless frontier settlers by the blood
thirsty savages.   Every succeeding hour
brought news of the rapid advance and
near approach of the Indians. It was time
that something should be done for the safety of the inhabitants. A meeting was called
and the situation was thoroughly discussed.
It was shown that the village was so surrounded by brush and timber that the Indians could approach unseen and surprise
the town, and that on account of this, and
the many ravines in which the foe con d
secrete themselves, it would be difficult for
the settlers to so fortify themselves in their
exposed situation, taking into consideration the small number of men, as to jus-
tify them in allowing the women and children to remain. After carefully considering the matter, it was decided to send the
women and children to a place of safety,
while the men would remain and if deemed
necessary they would build a fort and de-
fend themselves.

BUILD A STOCKADE.

Accordingly some of the women went to
Clearwater and some to St. Cloud, while
others joined their fortunes with the people of Maine Prairie. About fifteen men
stayed and fortified themselves by building a stockade around the old log building
that had been used as a hotel in the early
days of the village. Those that remained
armed themselves as best they could and
made the best preparations for a defense
possible. They organized by electing A.
Montgomery captain, and V. W. Olds
lieutenant. But before they had built
their fort a messenger had been sent from
Forest City, on the 19th day of August,
with the information that that town was
in great danger of being attacked by the
Indians, and asking the people of Fair
Haven to come to its assistance. Although
there was cause to fear that their own
town might be attacked while they were
absent, and the danger while going
through the timber was thought to be imminent, this did not deter them from the
undertaking. About a dozen men started
in the evening in wagons for Forest City.

It soon became so dark in the timber that
they could not see to follow the road, and
notwithstanding the fact that a ligh
would increase their danger by giving the
Indians the advantage if there should be
any lurking around, they were compelled
to light their lanterns and carry them
ahead of the teams. They arrived at
Kingston at day light and found the citizens of that place very much excited and
greatly alarmed. There were three or
four hundred refugees that had come in
from the surrounding country. They were
quartered in the grist mill and other
buildings. The little band from Fair
Haven here joined Capt. Adkins' company
of citizens. The alarm was caused by a
party of four Indians attacking some
whites at Acton. They had been hunting
in the neighborhood of that place for several days and appeared sullen and ugly.
However, as the Indians were at peace
with the whites no uneasiness has been
felt.

KILLING THE WHITES.

On Sunday, the 17th day of August,
these Indians came to the house of Mr.
Howard Baker. Visiting at their house
were their neighbors, Mr. Webster and
wife, and Mr. Jones and wife. The Indians seeing Mr. Jones, with whom they
had previously had a quarrel, wished to
renew it. They challenged Baker and
Jones to shoot at a mark. After shooting
they hastily reloaded their guns before the
whites had loaded theirs and began firing
at the whites, killing Mr. Jones and his
wife, and Baker and Webster. Miss Wilson was killed at Mr. Jones' house. Then,
stealing horses, this band of murderers
hastened back to their people near the
agency at Yellow Medicine. The next
day nearly all the Indians, who had been
waiting for some time at the agency for
their annual payments, which were con-
siderably over due, started off on the
war path to exterminate the whites, and
the most terrible massacre of settlers
ever known in the annals of frontier warfare was begun.

The party from Fair Haven, with Capt. Adkin's company, went to Forest City, then to Acton, but found that others had been there before them and had buried the dead. They then scouted around to Green Lake and other places to rescue any persons found alive, and to bury any found dead.

They returned to Forest City on Friday, the 22nd of August, and to Fair Haven the next day, without encountering the enemy. Although no Indians were seen near Fair Haven during the outbreak, it was believed that there were small scouting parties around. At one time, while J. G. Smith and two companions were working in the harvest field they distinctly heard some gun caps snapped in the brush near by. They quickly seized their guns and made an investigation, but found no one. They supposed that some Indians had tried to shoot them, but their guns had missed fire.

RETURNED TO THEIR HOMES.

The men that remained at Fair Haven slept in their fort nights and worked in their fields during the day. It was but two or three weeks before it was deemed safe for the women to return. Most of them came back to their homes and resumed their usual duties. But there was a feeling of uneasiness and fear until the winter, when it was believed that all danger was over.

BURYING THE DEAD.

Mr. John Goodspeed tells of his visit to Acton the next day, after Jones and his people were killed, when the coroner at Forest city empannelled a jury of 12 men men, including Mr. Goodspeed, to go to Acton to hold an inquest over the bodies of the slain, and bury the dead. They were accompanied by about 70 men on horseback At Mr. Howard Baker's house they found the dead bodies of Mr. Baker, Mr. Webster, Mr. Robinson Jones, and his wife. Going to the house of Mr. Jones they found his niece, a Miss Wilson, lying in the house dead. Her little sister was asleep when the tragedy occurred, and was covered with blood when found, for she had been vainly endeavoring to get her sister up. The bodies were not mutilated. They were all buried. While they were holding the inquest a party of 30 Indians appeared and were chased by those on horseback.

GERMAN SETTLEMENT.

There was a small settlement of Germans on the extreme northern line of the township of Fair Haven. One of the first of these to locate a claim was Henry Block. He was a native of Hanover, Germany, and, in the spring of 1856, came to this country and stopped a few months in Wisconsin. He then came to Fair Haven, and took a claim, which is situated on the shore of Beaver lake. His son H. C. still operates this same claim.

The other German families arrived several years later. During the Indian outbreak in 1862, several of these families fled to St. Cloud, but soon returned and all went to the house of Mr. Locher and fortified it as well as they could. In the day time they would venture out and secure their crops and sleep in the house nights, with some one to sit up and look out for Indians. One of this number narrates some alarms that they had, that, at the time, appeared very serious, but after the danger was over, and the causes of the alarm discovered, they could enjoy a good laugh over the incident.

"MIXING IT."

The long winter of 1862-3 passed quietly. The Indians had been driven back into the Dakota territory, and troops were stationed at Paynesville, Sauk Centre, on the Red River and at Chippewa, and supplies had to be hauled to them. Oats from Fair Haven and other towns were hauled to feed the horses at Chippewa, where the Government paid one dollar per bushel. Wheat could be bought for 50 cents per bushel, and one bushel of wheat would weigh nearly as much as two bushels of oats. It was a great temptation to those hauling oats to feed the Government horses and mules to mix some wheat with the oats. They could buy a bushel of wheat for fity cents and mix it with a bushel of oats that would cost forty cents and sell the mixture to the Government for nearly three bushels of oats. It was claimed that if the wheat was good, a pound of wheat was as valuable for feeding purposes as a pound of oats, and that the horses and mules were just as well suited with the mixture as with clear oats. It was only when the oats was mixed with foul seed, dirt,wild buckwheat and screenings that not only was the government cheated, but the animals were defrauded of their proper food. This demand for the farmers' produce assisted them greatly, and money, which for many years had been an almost unknown commodity, began to circulate.

KILLED BY INDIANS.

The spring came and with it quite active farming operations were begun in anticipation of good prices. Soon after the seeding was finished there were rumors that signs of Indians had been seen in the Big Woods and there was much uneasiness felt among the settlers of Fair Haven, and other adjoining towns. There were known to be small parties of Sioux prowling around in the timber south of the town, and the belief that they were hostile was fully confirmed by the tragic death of Henry McGannan, who was shot down by an unseen foe on the 28th day of June, on the road to Kingston. He was buried where he fell on the 1st of July, and in the fall the body was removed to the Fair Haven cemetery.

DESIGNING SOLDIERS

There were eight or ten soldiers from the 8th Minnesota Regiment stationed at Fair Haven that accompanied the mail back and forth from Kingston to this place as a guard, and also to scout wherever there was supposed to be danger from Indians. McGannan's death was succeeded by no other hostile demonstration, so, after a period of quiet, it began to be understood, (so tradition says) that the Government would soon send these troops South. Some of them did not relish this, and they set their wits to work to do something that would cause their being retained in their present position. It is claimed that three of them dressed up like Indians and went to the residence of Mrs. Hathaway, two or three miles west of the village, and finding her absent, and only her mother, Mrs. Storms, an old lady, at home, they pretended to be Indians and caught her and with a big knife cut off her hair and frightened her nearly to death. She escaped and fled to Fair Haven and reported that she had been attacked by Indians. This occasioned quite a panic among the people, and extra precautions were taken by the settlers to guard the women and children. A company of citizens was formed and the territory around that part of the country was thoroughly inspected for many days, these same soldiers assisting. But they had accomplished their object, for the Government, believing that there were Indians still around, the soldiers were kept at Fair Haven several months longer. It is told that one of the three who impersonated Indians at that time, has at this late day told the truth of the affair. McGannan was shot by Little Six and his son. Some time afterwards, Little Six and his son were shot at near Hutchinson, and the son killed. He had on McGannan's coat which would indicate that he was the murderer.

INDIANS STEAL HORSES.

Many signs of small parties of Sioux Indians had been observed in the towns of Fair Haven and Maine Prairie and as a result people were on the watch and many went armed. One Sunday afternoon in August, Christ Block who at that time was quite a young boy, discovered three Indians fishing in a small lake, called Beaver Lake, not far from his house, and informed his father of his discovery. About dark Mr. Block's horses came running from the pasture greatly frightened. Believing that the Indians had in some way been the cause of their alarm Mr. Block fastened them in his stable for a safety About twelve o'clock his dog began to bark in a furious manner, and Mr. Block went out and found three Indians leading his horses out of the stable. He was unarmed, but notwithstanding the odd of three to one he pitched into them and succeeded in driving them off and getting his horses and again secured them in the stable. The Indians ran for their guns, which they had left outside the yard and Block ran into the house for his gun. About two o'clock the Indians came back and Block, armed with a shot gun and his son Chris with a pistol, went out and opened fire on the Indians, who returned the fire, with the result on one side of a wounded Indian, on the other a bullet had passed through Block's cap. One shot had struck his gun and a stray ball had cut off the tail of a steer that was in the yard. The Indians retreated but soon returned and succeeded in getting away with two horses and a sucking colt. At daylight Mr. B. took their trail which went near Fair Haven. He was soon joined by the following State scouts. Quartus Farwell, Joseph Kimball, A. Farnsworth, B. F. Butler, A. W. Tucker, James Robinson, L. H. Brown and Elder Norris. These scouts followed the trail three days until they came out onto the prairie near Kingston. When near Albion the Indians killed a fine steer belonging to Mr. Holmes, and cut pieces of flesh out and took along with them. The scouts heard the firing, but it was near night and the trail could not be followed. The next morning when near Corrina, as the scouts emerged from the thick brush upon a march, they discovered the three Indians on the opposite side, dismounted. The Indians saw the scouts and sprang behind their horses, just as the scouts fired. They than sprang upon their horses and escaped into the thick brush, one of them reeling, as if badly wounded, and it was believed none escaped unhurt. In their haste they left a gun and two knives. When the horse thiefs reached

the prairie, word was sent to some cavalry and they pursued them thirty miles. There were but two Indians then and they escaped by swimming a lake. From the bloody clothing that they had left on the bank of the lake it was evident that both were wounded. The horses were returned to their owner, but in a wretched used up condition.

Soon after this the scouting parties of Indians left for their safer hunting grounds in the far west and there was a feeling of relief among the settlers.

The winter of 1864, will long be remembered for its changeable weather. On the 2nd and 3d of January the the thermometer showed 42 degrees below zero, while on the 20th it was 70 degrees above, a difference of of 112 degrees. It is the custom in Minnesota for the farmers to kill their beef and pork in the fall or early winter and let the meat freeze and keep it frozen until toward Spring or until a better price is obtainable. This meat will keep fresh and good generally until Spring but the extremely warm weather this winter caused it to thaw out and much of the meat was ruined on account of the continued warm weather.

The next year, 1864, was a quiet one as far as any startling incident to Fair Haven is concerned. The old settlers do not remember anything worthy of note that occurred that year only the deep interest taken by this patriotic town in the war of the southern rebellion where so many of her sons were fighting for their country. More volunteers were needed and it had been decided by the general government to raise them by draft if they could get them in no other way. Then came the perplexing question of how to draft men and from what districts, for some towns had sent more men than others according to their population. In the first part of the war but little attention was paid to the subject of crediting each man to the town that he lived in, but when the town of Fair Haven was credited up with her volunteers it showed that more than the town's quota had volunteered and consequently there would be no draft in that town. This was a matter of pride in the town and also of rejoicing. The draft was set for January 4th, 1864, but before that date so many had volunteered that it was postponed.

From the St. Cloud *Democrat* of March 10th, 1864, the following items of interest concerning Fair Haven are gleaned:

"The quotas of the following towns are given showing how many volunteers had been credited to that town and how many were her share to send. They are given for all calls from the commencement of the war to the this time: Fair Haven's quota was 18 and she has furnished 25, showing that this town is 7 ahead of her quota. Maine Prairie's quota was 20 and she has furnished 25 Lynden's quota was 16 and she has furnished 15."

The following sad announcement is found under date of March 10th:

"Mr. James Tucker, of Fair Haven, who was working in the pineries in the camp of F. Morrison, was killed by a limb from a falling tree striking him on the head. He lived eleven hours after the accident."

July 1st O. D Webb got the contract to carry the mail from St. Cloud to Fair Haven via Maine Prairie once a week: leaving St. Cloud at 6 a. m. Tuesday; arriving at Fair Haven at 12 m and returning to St. Cloud at 7 p. m. of the same day.

The spring 1865 was a season of rejoicing to the people of Fair Haven. The news of the surrender of General Lee and his army to General Grant caused much rejoicing in the hearts of those who had friends and relatives in the army, and they looked forward with pleasant anticipation to the time in the near future when the boys in blue would return home and peace should reign over a united and prosperous nation. It was but a few days after receiving the glad tidings of Lee's surrender that the appalling news of the assasination of President Abraham Lincoln was heralded through the land. This intelligence cast a deep gloom over the whole country and grave fears were entertained that it might lead to a continuation of the war or the breaking up of the nation into several different governments. But the intelligence sound sense and understanding of the people prevented such a catastroph, and, soon, peace was assured.

Until the year 1865, there were but few settlers in the northern and eastern part of the town of Fair Haven, and a large part of the town was covered with brush and timber, but about this time this land began being settled upon and improved. Claims began to be taken and improved in the timber to the south and west. This summer Grinols & Cooper opened a store of general merchandise and did a thriving business. About this time it was discovered that immense quantities of ginseng grew in the timber in the vicinity of Fair Haven. The people turned out and dug the root and an immense traffic soon began with this valuable product. The roots were shipped to China. It was stated that from sixty thousand to eighty thousand dollars were paid out for the root in one season, a large part of it was bought by Grinols & Cooper, and although it seemed as if every foot of ground was searched each year, it was many years before it ceased to be profitable to hunt for genseng at certain seasons of the year.

With the war of the rebellion over, with good crops and good prices the people of Fair Haven began to see bright prospects ahead, and to forget the many privations that they had passed through. The store of Grinols & Cooper, as well as the grist mill, brought many people there to trade, or to get their wheat ground into flour. The saw mill was well patronized and many hauled logs to the mill to be converted into lumber, and nearly every day in the year the streets were thronged with people from the country, some of them coming a distance of ten to fifteen miles.

PRICES COMPARED.

In order to show how the prices of farm

products fluctuate and also to show the prices paid for groceries, the following market reports are taken from the St. Cloud *Democrat* of March 20th, May 3d, and Sept. 1865, and from the St. Cloud DAILY TIMES of October, 1895. Although good prices were received for farm produce in 1865, yet for everything that they bought a correspondingly high price was paid. Sugar, tea and kerosene were exceedingly high. Here are the figures:

	March 20 1865.	May 3 1865.	Sept. 1865.	Oct. 1865.
Wheat per bu	$1 25	$0 80	$0 60	$0 50
Corn " "	1 25	1 00	75	15
Oats " "	65	85	45	20
Rye " "	1 15	1 15	50	
Barley " "	1 60	1 30	—	—
Beans " "	4 00	3 00	2 50	1 25
Onions " "	5 00	5 00	—	50
Hay per ton	8 00	7 00	6 00	5 00
Eggs per doz	20	12½	20	12½
Pork per cwt	15 00	15 00	15 00	—
Kerosene per gal.	1 50	1 30	1 20	15
Flour per barrel	9 75	8 00	—	3 30
Sugar per pound	.26@ 37	16@ 26	17@ 25	06
Tea per lb	1 50@ 2 50	1 25	1 25@ 2 00	50

NO NOTABLE EVENTS.

There were not many notable events occuring in Fair Haven during the year 1866. John K. Noyes had the contract for carrying the mail from St. Cloud to Fair Haven, and in July a tri-weekly mail route was established from Clearwater to Forest City, through Fair Haven and Kingston. Prior to this year school had been taught in such buildings as could be hired, but a school house was built that year which answered all purposes for a short time. Soon however, the increase of the population demanded a more commodious building and in 1880 the present fine school building was completed.

On the first of September the railroad was completed from St. Paul to St. Cloud and there was much rejoicing in consequence.

The crops, this year were fine, and the usual sequence of nature's prodigality was observable in this little village in the mating of the young people.

We copy from the St. Cloud *Democrat*, of May 24th 1866, the following notices of the wedding of two of Fair Haven's popular young men to two of Fair Haven's fair daughters:

"At the residence of T. C. Partridge, Rev. T. C. Partridge united in the holy bonds of matrimony James B. Vandervoort to Miss Valona M. Partridge."

"May 24, 1886, at the residence of O. D. Webb, by Rev. J. N. Thresher, Mr. R. M. Vandervoort to Miss Alma Webb."

The fine Octagon hotel belonging to and operat d by J. K. Noy· s was destroyed in the fall of this year. It was a great loss to the village as well as to Mr. Noyes.

JUNE FRESHET, 1867.

In the June freshet of 1867, the waters in the Clearwater river were greatly swollen, and the mills and dam at Fair Haven were in great danger of being swept away. Everything was done to strengthen the dam and prevent the threatened catastrophe, but all in vain. With a mighty roar the huge volume of water began pouring over the dam, and in an incredibly short time the flouring mill and dam were swept down the river. The loss was keenly felt, not only by the owners, but by the whole community. But with their characteristic energy and enterprise the owners, Messrs. J. A. Linscott and Wm. Vie, immediately began to rebuild the dam and mill, and had it rebuilt and running that same year. This was an unlucky year for Fair Haven. Besides the loss of the flouring mill, Grinola & Cooper's store was burned. But they were soon established in a new building.

FAIR HAVEN CHURCHES.

The Christian church was organized in 1886, and in the year 1887 the organization erected their present house of worship, which was dedicated on the 4th day of September of that year. The dedicatory services were performed by Elder Pier, of Litchfield, and Elder Campbell, of Howard Lake, preached the sermon at the first quarterly meeting. Elder Truax was their first minister, and preached for two years. The organization started out with 23 members. Soon 35 new members were added. Since Sept. 1st, 1893, there has been no church organization.

The Seventh Day Advent church was

organized April 26, 1879. Its first officers were Mr. S. Gregory, Elder; S. Leavitt, Deacon, and John Donehoe, clerk. In 1889 their present house of worship was built and was dedicated by W. H. Tenny. The church was organized by W. B Hill, a Seventh Day Adventist minister.

The Methodist Episcopal church building of Fair Haven was built in 1889. The building is 24 feet wide by 40 feet long, will seat about two hundred people, and cost $1,100 Its first trustees were Adam Ringer, P. P Partridge, and C M. King. It was dedicated by the presiding Elder, John Stafford, and had twenty-five members at that time. The following persons have held the office of trustee in later years: John Goodspeed Arnold Goodspeed and S. C. Kemp. It has had as pastors Thomas E. Archer, C. E. Powell and John Doran.

The present Baptist church was built in 1868.

G. A. R. HALL.

The Grand Army Hall was built in 1889. The funds to build it with were raised by subscription besides labor was donated by the members of the Post.

CLOSE OF NARRATIVE.

This completes the present early history of the now prosperous and growing town of Fair Haven. The main idea of the writer has been to show how the people lived in a new coun'ry; the many privations they had to endure, and how bravely and hopefully they persevered and overcame the obstacles that confronted them in their new homes. The memory of the early settlers has had to be relied upon for most of the incidents related in this work. The good people of Fair Haven have done everything in their power to assist in this work, and the writer takes this opportunity to thank them for the many favors shown him, and to ask them to overlook the many mistakes that must necessarily be made when the memory of thirty-five to forty years ago is depended upon for information.

BIOGRAPHICAL SKETCHES.

I append a few biographical sketches of Fair Haven's earliest pioneers.

THOMAS C. PARTRIDGE.

Thomas C. Partridge the first discoverer and founder of the townsite of Fair Haven was born near Pittsburg, Penn., in 1815. His parents moved to Trumball county, Ohio. In the fall of 1854, he came to Minnesota and built a house in Minneapolis. The next spring he traded this home for a farm, 9 miles northwest of Minneapolis, which he farmed for two years. In the spring of of 1856, he, with a few men discovered Fair Haven, and located it as a townsite, and had it surveyed and platted that summer. In the fall he brought up his wife and family, consisting of Payson P., Cecil, Florus and daughter Valona. Mr. Partridge was a Free Baptist He built a large log house and that winter religious meetings were held in his house, and for many years he preached in that and surrounding towns. He took a great deal of interest in town and school boards and used his influence for an economical management of public affairs. His daughter Valona married J. B. Vandervort May 23, 1866. Florous B. Partridge married Miss Anna Hurtz Oct. 3, 1880.

JOHN L. DEAN.

John L. Dean was born in Ohio, and came to Fair Haven in May 1856, and took a claim. He engaged in farming and carpenting for some time and then became agent for Holmes & Tyler, nurserymen. Mr. Dean and Miss Sarah Tucker were married at Fair Haven, in 1858. Their children were named Hettie, Elida, Albert Frederick, Louise and Florence. He died in 1884.

LOVINUS ABELL.

Lovinus Abell was one of the party that first discovered Fair Haven, in the spring of 1856. He was b rn in Trumball county, Ohio, in 1809. He took a claim and built a house. In the fall he was joined by his wife and daughters, Jane and Laurie, and sons Newton, Westley, John and Milton. Mr. Abell was a farmer all his life. In 1884 he passed quietly away at the age of 75 years. His wife, who is 84 ye·rs old, is still quite active, with her intellectual faculties as clear as ever, and remembers many incidents of their pioneer life.

Of the children, John and Milton are now living in Fair Haven, and Jane is now Mrs. L. Belden and also living in Fair Haven. Westley, Newton and Laurie have passed over the silent river.

JOHN G. SMITH.

John G. Smith was born in Trumbull county, Ohio, in 1834, and worked on a farm until the fall of 1855, when he came to Minnesota In the spring of 1856 he was one of the first to discover the place where the village of Fair Haveen now stands, and took a claim May 28, about one mile north of it. He has resided on this farm ever since. He was married in 1871, and has ten children living. He has been a member of the town board several years, and was prominent in town affairs. He came from the Wester Reserve, Ohio. When he lived there Garfield was their representative in congress. At a time when congress had voted a censure upon Joshua Giddings, Mr. Smith took an active part in the canvass for his re-election, and at one time drove him 12 miles to speak at a mass meeting. Mr. Giddings was elected to congress that fall.

D. A. PERKINS.

D. A. Perkins was born in Canada, in 1834, and in 1839 he moved to Pennsylvania· He also lived in Ohio awhile and came from that State to Minnesota in 1854, and stopped at Minneapolis until 1857, when he arrived at Fair Haven He enlisted in Co. C. 1st Minnesota Regiment in 1861, and was discharged in 1864, and re-enlisted in the same regiment and served until the close of the war. He was captured June 22, 1864, before Petersburg and was a prisoner nine months, parts of the time he was confined in the Andersonville, Libby, Bell Island and Florence prisons. He remained in Fair Haven until 1867, when he went to work on his farm

near Sauk Center. He has resided in St. Cloud fifteen years. He was married in Jan. 1867.

JOHN GOODSPEED.

In 1856 John Goodspeed visited Maine Prairie, but soon went to Manannah. In 1866, he came to Fair Haven, and settled on a farm which he had bought five years before. He has operated this farm ever since, in an intelligent and skillful manner. He has taken great interest in the affairs of his town, and has served as chairman of supervisors nine years, and several years as supervisor as well as being on the school board. He was born in Kennebec county, Maine, in 1833, and came to Minnesota in 1854, and located at Minneapolis. In 1859, Mr. Goodspeed and Miss Helen Bryant were married. They were accompanied to Fair Haven with three children, Eunice, Frank and Alvin.

JOSEPH H. LOCKE.

Joseph H. Locke was born in Holowell, Maine, in 1820. He was brought up in the mercantile business, which he followed in Boston, Massachusetts, until 1849, when he went to California and spent several years in mining. He then returned to the states. In 1857 he came to Minnesota and located in the town of Fair Haven, where he bought a farm and resided upon it until he moved to St. Cloud in 1884. Mr. Locke and Miss Martha B. Bradford were married in 1845. They adopted two children, Fanny W. and Harry S. Mr. Locke was a member of the Unitarian church of St. Cloud. On the 31st of January, 1891, he quietly passed to the other side of the river. His wife, who is 73 years of age, still survives him. His adopted son, H. S. Locke, is now a well known attorney in St. Cloud.

O. D. WEBB.

O. D. Webb was born in Jefferson county, New York, in July, 1821. At the age of eighteen he left home and worked for two years in a flouring mill. He then went to Plainsfield, Illinois, and afterward to Chicago, and was clerk in a store one year. He then traveled through the northwest, and visited the east and returned to Plainsfield, where he built and run a flouring mill In 1855 he came to Minnesota, locating at Sauk Rapids, where he built a saw mill and afterwards added a flouring mill. He built and operated flouring mills at Fair Haven, Paynesville and at Clifton, Wis. In 1878 he moved to Melrose, and in 1885 he returned to Fair Haven. In 1886 had a stroke of paralysis which was the cause of his death that year. Mr. Webb was married on the 4th of April, 1847, to Miss Esther Northup, of Lewis county, New York. When he returned to Fair Haven he was accompanied by his wife and three daughters, Alma, Ella and Emma.

BENJAMIN GRINOLS.

Benjamin Grinols was born in the town of Osto, New York, in 1832. His early life was spent on a farm. He came to Anoka county, Minnesota, in 1856, and farmed it until in the summer of 1865, when he arrived in Fair Haven and engaged with Wm. Cooper as partner, in the business of general merchandise. Mr. Mr. Grinols and Miss Isabelle Cooper were married in May, 1859. Their three children are Clinton D., Ernest E. and Elsie J. All are married. On account of the death of his partner, Wm. Cooper, Mr. Grinols formed a company known as Grinols & Sons, with his sons Clinton D. and E. E. as partners. In 1887 they sold out their merchandise business to Strout & Sons, and went into the business of farm machinery.

WILLIAM COOPER.

In 1856 Wm Cooper arrived in Fair Haven, and engaged in the business of general merchandise in company with Benjamin Grinols. Mr. Cooper was born in Philadelphia, Pa., in March, 1838 He moved with his family into the northern part of the State when five years of age. He followed farming until 1857, when he came to Minnesota and settled in Anoka county. In 1862 he enlisted in the Eighth Minnesota Volunteer Infantry, and served eighteen months on the frontier in pursuit of the Indians, and then went south, but after six months was discharged on account of wounds received at the battle of Murfreesboro. He was Postmaster of Fair Haven for a number of years. On the 20th day of May, 1866, Mr. Cooper and Mrs. Lizzie Robinson, daughter of J R. Noyes, were married. The names of their children are Minnie M., Maud A. and Blanche. He died Feb. 24th, 1882.

C. J. BOOBAR.

Mr. C. J. Boobar was one of the prominent men of Fair Haven. He was born in Milo, Maine, in 1811, and when old enough, he engaged in the lumber business. He was married in 1836, and in 1858 he came to Minnesota, from the town of Lee, Maine, accompanied by his wife and a large family. He was elected one of the first justices of the peace in the town of Fair Haven. He took a deep interest in the affairs of the town, school and literary society. In 1872, he quietly passed over the silent river, leaving a wife and large family of children besides hosts of friends to mourn his loss His wife is now (1895) in good health with faculties as bright as many younger women. She is 79 years old.

STEPHEN SIAS.

Stephen Sias was born in Wyoming county, N. Y., April 19, 1830, and lived on a farm there until 1860. He married Mrs. Desire Baldwin, sister of Benjamin Grinols, of Fair Haven, in 1855. In 1856 he came to Minnesota an l settled in Anoka county. In 1861, he moved to Anoka, and worked at the cooper trade until 1865, when he came to Fair Haven, and remained unt l 1889. While at Fair Haven he was engaged in farming, coopering and carpentering. His wife died in 1889. He then moved to Eden Valley where he lived until his death, which occurred in 1893. His only son, Frank L, is now engaged in the lumber business in Eden Valley. Mr. Sias' step-son, Jerome Baldwin, enlisted from Fair Haven, in 1865, and died in the army. Mr. Sias first came to

Fair Haven in 1860, but on account of the Indian scare went back to Anoka.

A. FARNSWORTH.

A. Farnsworth was born in Cherryfield, Maine, in 1840. In 1861 he enlisted in the Birdan Sharp Shooters and served two years, and came to Fair Haven in 1862. He engaged in the lumbering business until 1872, when he bought a farm of Richard Rice. His wife died that spring and he went to Minneapolis and remained there eight years, when he returned to his farm, where he has remained ever since. In 1879 he married again. They have two children. In 1863 he joined the State scouts and scouted around Fair Haven, and was one of those that pursued the three Indians that stole Block's horses.

S. C. STROUT.

S. C. Strout was born in Maine in 1833, and went to Wisconsin in 1855 and engaged in farming. In 1865 he moved to Maine Prairie, and in 1867 he settled in Fair Haven, where he operated a farm until 1874, when he engaged in the mercantile business for two years, and kept a hotel one year. He moved to Monticello, where he remained until 1887. He and his son, Fred L., then engaged in the mercantile business in Fair Haven until his death in 1893. His son, Fred L., sold out the store and moved to Paynesville.

WM. H. DAY.

Wm. H. Day was born in the town of Cushing, Kennebec county, Maine, in 1821, and arrived in Fair Haven in 1856, remaining there four years. In 1860 he moved onto a farm in Maine Prairie. He was the first constable elected when the three towns were organized into one town. He was also a member of the Board of Supervisors. His son Eugene, was the first white child born in Fair Haven, which occurred in 1857. He tilled his farm for many years. In Maine he followed farming and lumbering. Mr. Day assisted in building the first house built on the Fair Haven town site in the fall of 1856.

R. M. VANDERVORT.

Richard M. Vandervort was born in Clinton county, Ohio, in 1842. He came from there to Fair Haven in 1861, and for sixteen years was engaged in the mercantile business in that place. Mr. Vandervort has taken a great deal of interest in town, county and national affairs, and has been prominent in business connected with the improvement of the town. He also took a deep interest in the cause of education, and the improvement of the schools. He held the office of town clerk for ten years and has held some town office almost continually. In 1862 he was one of the party of fifteen that went to the assistance of Forest City, upon the first of the Indian outbreak. He also took a prominent part in connection with the fort life with the people of Maine Prairie in 1862.

H. P. BENNETT.

H. P. Bennett was born in Spencer, Massachusetts, in 1819, and when 12 years old he went to Chicopee, where he was engaged in making patterns for a foundry. In 1857 he came to Maine Prairie and bought a farm and carried it on until 1863 when he moved to St. Cloud, and opened a gun store and repair shop. In 1888 his wife died. He soon after sold out his store and retired to private life. He was one of the first collectors in the town and also held the office of Justice of the Peace several years.

WILLARD C. TUFTS

Willard C. Tufts was born in Massachusetts in 1836, and moved to Illinois in 1856, remaining there one year. He then came to Fair Haven, took a claim which he farmed until 1861, when he enlisted in Company D, 4th Minnesota Regiment, and served four years. He then returned and bought a farm three miles from the village and tilled it fourteen years. He then located on a farm west of the village, where he now resides. Mr. Tufts married Elvira Smith. Their children's names are John and Carrie.

HENRY BLOCK.

Henry Block was born in Hanover, Germany, in 1812. He and Miss Johanna Ziegenbein were married in 1842. In 1856 be came to this country, stopping a few months in Wisconsin. He started with his family in an ox team and arrived near the north line of Fair Haven on the 15th of September. Here his wagon broke down, and he located his claim near there on Beaver Lake. He was accompanied by his wife and two sons, H. C. and Henry. His son H. C. now owns and operates this farm.

JOHN K. NOYES.

John K. Noyes was born in Jonesborough, Maine, in 1817. His principal occupation was lumbering until 1856, when he came to Fair Haven. He built an octogan hotel, and operated it a number of years and in the meantime improved and carried on his farm. He was also engaged for a number of years in building dams. Mr. Noyes took a deep interest in the affairs of the town and county, and was quite prominent in developing the resources of the town. He took a leading part in organizing the Old Settlers' Association of the towns of Maine Prairie and Fair Haven, and making their meetings interesting. Mr. Noyes and Miss Martha Small were married in Maine. He was accompanied to Fair Haven by his wife and daughters Josephine, Elizabeth, Mary, Bernice, Laurie and Julia, and sons George M. and Frank L. Mr. Noyes died Dec. 7th, 1883, and Mrs. Noyes followed him April 23d, 1893.

MRS. GEO. R. WHITNEY.

Among the early settlers was Mrs. Geo. R. Whitney. She was born in Maine in 1821, and was married in 1838. In the spring of 1857 the family came to Minnesota. Her husband started from their home in Maine a few days before the family, intending to transact some business in Boston and then join the family as they came along, but was taken suddenly sick and died and was buried by his friends before the family arrived. The wife came on with her family consisting of her one A. J., Alverton, Geo. R., Horace and F. H., and daughter Mary A. The family resided for one year nine miles above Minneapolis and in March, 1858, moved to Fair Haven. Mrs. Whitney and D. A. Hoyt, were married in 1859 and moved on to Mr. Hoyt's farm on Maine Prairie. In 1886 they were divorced and in 1889, she married Sylvanus Jenkins. Of the children A. J. married Miss Ellen Clark and lived on Maine Prairie and kept store a number of years He was Second Lieutenant of Company D, 4th Minnesota Regiment. He died in June, 1884. Horace was drowned in the big flood near Bismarck in the spring of 1876. Alverton died in the army at Chattanoog April 23, 1865. Geo. R. is in business at Sauk Center. F. H. is engineer at the Reformatory at St. Cloud. The daughter, Mary A., is Mrs. W. H. Thompson, of St. Cloud.

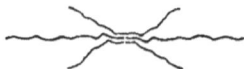

History of Lynden.

By E. H. ATWOOD.

ITS LOCATION.

The town of Lynden is situated in the southeast corner of Stearns county, and is mostly covered with brush and timber. A large part of the town is undulating, with a rich and fertile soil. The Mississippi river forms its eastern boundary while the Clearwater river flows along its southern line. A few settlers arrived in the town in 1853, but it was not until 1856 that any considerable settlement was made. The town is so situated that its history is very intimately connected with the towns of Clearwater and St. Cloud. The settlers of Lynden received their mail and attended church, bough their supplies and sold their produce at these points. For many years the settlers occupied only the eastern side of the town, and a large part of the western side of the town remained unsettled.

BUT FEW OLD SETTLERS REMAIN.

There are now but few of the early settlers living in the town. Some have died, and others have moved away There has been but little of an exciting nature in the history of the town.

LYNDEN WAR VOLUNTEERS.

During the rebellion, the town furnished its quota of volunteers for the army, and her sons did noble work on many southern battle fields. The farmers were an intelligent, active and progressive class of citizens, and conducted their farming opera-

tions in an enlightened and business-like manner. During the early years of the town's existence, the settlers saw hard times, and scant fare, and suffered many privations. The following are among the names of those who enlisted during the war: Carroll H. Clifford, Frank W. Clifford, George C. Clifford, John W. Lyons, William H. Lyons, James M. Lyons, E. P. Parcher, Frank M. Parcher, Benjamin Robinson, Adam Bunt, William Dallas, Wilber F. Fisk, James Langdon, C. H. Vorse and George T. Campbell. There was one lacking to fill the town's quota, and Levi Gleason was drafted and afterward promoted to chaplain. All of the above named volunteers lived and returned to their homes, except E. P. Parcher, who was killed at the battle of The Cedars December 7th, 1864.

THE FIRST SETTLERS.

It is claimed that John Townsend made the first claim in the town, in 1853 He was a native of Pennsylvania. William and John McDonald and Joseph and Peter Townsend arrived the same year, and the next year took claims. In 1854, Jonathan and Wm. Dallas arrived, and located in the town. They were natives of Indiana. M. D. Campbell came from Ohio, and Jas. Campbell, his brother, from the State of New York, and took claims that fall. The next year J. W. Stevenson and Abell Kent arrived in the town, from Ohio, and took

claims in section nine and ten. Mr. Kent
was accompanied by his wife, and four
daughters. Geo. T. Cambell also arrived
and took a claim this year.

THE FIRST MARRIAGE— A SCARE.

In the fall of 1855, J W. Stevenson and
Miss Emma Kent, were joined in the holy
bonds of matrimony. As there was no
officer qualified to perform the ceremony
on the west side of the Mississippi river,
it was necessary to go across the river.
Simon Stevens lashed two Indian canoes
together and took the wedding party over
the river. As the party was quite large
it took several trips. When the party arrived on the opposite bank, a boy was dis-
patc ed for John Steveson, a Justice of the
Peace in the then county of Benton. The
place where they were is now in Sher-
burne county, Benton county having been
divid d. The bride and groom were accompanied by their relatives and a few invited guests. But, as is usual in such
cases, many of the young men were not
invited to witness the ceremony, and felt
agrieved at being thus slighted, and concluded to see the performance, invitation
or no invitation. While the bridal party
was waiting upon the eastern bank of the
father of waters for the arrival of the one
man in all that vast region clothed with
the authority to legally join them together, standing upon ground that had
probably never before been pressed by the
foot of the white man, surrounded by a
primeval forest that had never been despoiled by the advancing tide of civiliza-
tion, the young uninvited men had quietly crossed over the river and surrounded
the bridal party and secreted themselves
in the brush where they could see the
ceremony and not be seen themselves.
Soon the "Squire" came and began the
ceremony. He had never before been
called upon for such a purpose It was
new business to him, but he finally pro-
nounced them man and wife. Th s was
the signal agreed upon by the uninvited,
and they simultaneously sprang up, fired
off their guns and gave the Indian war

whoop. All of the bridal party were badly
frightened, and the terrible shock caused
some of the women to faint.

Geo. T. Cambell came from Boston in
1855, and bought a claim and remained
one year, then returned to Boston, but
came back in 1860. That same fall Joseph
Townsand and Miss Harriet Ball, of Lynden, were married. They also had to cross
the Mississippi river to have the ceremony
properly performed. In March, 1858, A
B. Darby and Jerusha Ingalls were married and were the first couple to have the
ceremony performed in the town of Lynden.

ARRIVALS IN 1856.

Among the arrivals in 1856 were A. S.
Clifford, Truman Parcher, L. C. Johnson, Geo. E. Warner, Martin Johnson,
Stephen Oyster, E. G. Mathews, T
Heaton, A. C. Powers, E. G. Mat-
thews, and B. T. Lyons. They
took claims in the eastern part of the town.
The same year Charles Dally, Joseph
Pratt and Mr. McCooney settled on the
west side of the town, near Fair Haven.
Mr. Dally operated his claim until his
death about the year 1880. Mr. Pratt
moved to Nebraska about the year 1873
Mr. McConney remained but a few years
on his claim.

CLEARWATER'S FATAL BLUNDER

The destinies of man, as well as of towns,
cities and even nations, are often changed
by events that seem at the time of very
little importance. History is replete with
apparently unimportant events that have
turned the tide of battles or the fate of nations. Cities have grown to immense pro-
portions in spite of unfavorable natural
conditions, while at other places, where
everything in nature points to it as a suitable site for a great metropolis, a stragling
town is found. Some of the early settlers
of Clearwater think that a very small
event changed the career of that place and
prevented it from now occupying the
proud position of the "Fourth City" of
Minnesota. In 1856, the Burbank stage
company were running their stages from

St. Paul to the Red River of the North, by way of St. Cloud, as well as hauling supplies over this route. They found that by making a road from Clearwater to Cold Spring it would save 12 to 15 miles of travel over the sandy road from Clearwater to St. Cloud. The saving of this distance was a big item to the company, with their heavy traffic They made a proposition to the townsite owners of Clearwater, offering to make a good road from that place to Cold Spring, through the rich and fertile towns of Fair Haven, Maine Prairie and Luxemburg, providing that, in return, they were to have sufficient land for their barns, stables and warehouses. They intended to make this place a base of operations. The boats could bring up their supplies from St. Anthony during the whole season of navigation, whereas, it was only during the high water that the boats could reach St. Cloud. The road to Cold Spring would run through a very fertile country, now fast settling up, and soon immense quantities of wheat, corn and oats would be hauled to Clearwater and sold to be shipped by boat to St. Anthony, and the money for the grain would be spent in the town for supplies that would be brought up by water at a rate cheaper than it could be hauled by team, as the case was at Saint Cloud. Consequently, the farmers could get better prices at Clearwater for their supplies. Then, again, the immense trains of Red River carts that made annual trips to S. Cloud and St. Paul would come by way of Cold Spring to Clearwater, and as they could send their goods down on the boat and get their supplies up from St. Paul cheaper than they could to go down with their trains, this town would become the terminal point of these trains This alone would be a big item. This, together with the vast fertile country to the southwest with unlimited quantities of the various kinds of hard wood for lumber and manufacturing purposes, and together with a splendid water power, capable of running two flouring mills and a saw mill, would naturally point out this place as having all that was needed of natural advantages to make in the near future, a large and flourishing city. But, the townsite owners, like many others in the early days, were short sighted, and replied to the Burbank Company's proposition, that their lots were for sale, but not to give away. The result was that the road to Cold Spring was never opened, and the company continued to go by way of St. Cloud.

FIRST BIRTH—FIRST DEATH.

The first child born in the town was a son of Peter Townsand. He was named Byron in August, 1856.

J. W. Stevenon, who was the first to marry in the town was the first to die. His death occurring on the 14th day of September, 1856.

LYNDEN'S MILLS.

A mill was built at the mouth of the Clearwater river in 1856, but before starting up a flood washed it away. A steam saw mill was erected and operated in 1857 by Frank Morrison. Stephen Oyester was the millwright who built the mill. Thos. C. Rogers built the lower flouring mill in 1858, and in 1860 James Cambell erected the upper flouring mill and operated it several years.

FIRST SCHOOL.

The first school was taught in a shanty in the winter of 1858-59, by J. Kingsley, from Vermont. The first school house was built in 1859, the funds for building it were raised by subscription. The first teacher in the new house was Marrietta Vorse.

FIRST ELECTION.

The first election was held in the house of S. A. Clifford in October, 1857. It was then called Clearwater precinct. S. A. Clifford, Truman Parcher and Martin Johnson were judges of election, and A. C. Powers and W. D. Davis were clerks. A preliminary meeting of the voters of the town to consider the question of organizing the town was held in 1858. The settlers were few and the town was not organized until Jan. 15th, 1859.

ORGANIZING THE TOWN

The citizens had petitioned the county commissioners for an order to form a town. The petition was granted and the voters notified to meet on the 15th day of January, 1859, and organize by electing the necessary officers. The notice from the county commissioners was signed by T. C. McClure as clerk of the board. At the first town meeting S. A. Clifford, T. Parcher and A. Kent were chosen judges of election. The county commissioners had designated the name of the town "Croning," but the voters christened it Lynden. The following officers were elected as the first officers of the new town: Supervisors, Seth Gibbs, chairman; Martin Johnson and Truman Parcher; W. A. Sumner, town clerk; T. Heaton and F. H. Thompson, constables; W. P. Rigby and John McDonald, justice of the peace; S. A. Clifford, assessor; overseer of the poor, N. W. Merrill; road overseer, Jonathan Sargent; T. Heaton, collector.

GRANGE OF P. OF H.

In October, 1873, a Grange of the Patrons of Husbandry was organized by Mr. Parsons, master of the State Grange. W. T. Rigby was elected master; T. C. Porter, overseer; Geo. E. Warner, chaplain; James Baxter, lecturer; W. J. Hicks, gate keeper; G. Winslow, steward; B. Bosworth, assistant steward; John Oaks, secretary. Mrs. Rigby, Mrs. Kirk, Mrs. Bosworth and Mrs. Baxter were elected to fill the ladies' offices.

FIRST MASONIC LODGE   CEMETERY

1. October, 1858, a masonic lodge was organized. The first officers were: W. M., T. C. Rogers; S. W., J. M. Mitchell; J. W., S. Chenard; Treas. and W. W. Webster, Sec. At a meeting of the lodge on the 20th of October, 1866, upon the suggestion of W. T. Rigby, a committee was appointed to select suitable grounds for a cemetery. The committee reported on the 3d of November following, and were instructed to file articles of incorporation for the lodge, and in its name to purchase five and five-sixteenths acres of land in section thirty-four, and to have it surveyed and platted for a burial place, under the name of Acassia cemetery. This was the first ground dedicated to that purpose between Monticello and St. Cloud. Through the influence of this lodge, they have a beautiful cemetery with grounds well kept, an honor to the lodge and town. They have added to the original plat until now they have about 20 acres. It should be an incentive to other towns to follow the noble example of this society and town. This organization may well feel proud of the fruits of their labors.

ACKNOWLEDGMENT.

For much of the early history of Lynden, the writer is indebted to, and has taken extracts from the History of the Mississippi Valley published in 1881. The chapter in that work, giving the facts as to Lynden, was, undoubtedly, very largely the work of the Hon. W. T. Rigby, who was one of the early settlers and was prominent in town, county and state affairs.

This will end the early history of this town. Many thanks to those who have assisted in this work.

B. T. LYONS.

B. T. Lyons was one of the early settlers of Lynden. He was born in Virginia in 1813, near where the famous battle of Bull Run was afterwards fought. In 1840 he moved to Ohio and from there to Illinois in 1854. In 1856 he moved to Lynden, accompanied by his wife and six sons. He took a claim and operated it until his death, which occurred in 1889. He held the office of constable for a number of years. His six sons Wm. H., John W., Robert A., James N., Jacob H. and D. F. are all living at the present time (1895) excepting John W., who died in 1887. Two of the sons, James N. and John W. were in the army during the rebellion. Wm. H., Robt. A., James N. and D. F. are farming in Lynden. Jacob H. is farming in Fair Haven.

GEORGE E. WARNER.

George E. Warner was born in the province of Quebec. He came to Clearwater in the spring of 1856. He first took a claim on Maine Prairie, but sold it to Moses Ireland, and took a claim in Lynden, which he has cultivated ever since. His wife joined him in 1857. He held the office of chairman of supervisors for eight years and justice of the peace for a number of years. He has been one of Lynden's successful farmers.

T. HEATON.

T. Heaton was born in Waterbury, Vermont, and came to Minnesota in 1856. He began that fall building the house he now occupies. He has held the office of chairman of supervisors for a number of years. He has engaged in farming and operated a threshing machine several years. He has a wife and five children. Mr. H. is of a long lived family. His mental faculties are still clear. He was born in 1812.

GEORGE T. CAMBELL.

George T Cambell was born in Boston, Mass., in 1835. His principal occupation was carpentering, which he followed in New York and several other states. He came from Boston to Lynden in 1855, and took a claim, then returned to New York and remained until the fall of 1861. In August, 1862, he enlisted in Co. E, 8th Minnesota Regiment and served one year, guarding the frontier against the Indians. In the spring of 1864 he was with General Sully's expedition against the Indians, and went south that fall. Mr. Cambell and Miss Mattie W. Whittemore were married in 1866. They have two children.

ALVIN TOWNSEND.

Alvin Townsend was born in Pennsylvania in 1821. He came to the town of Lynden in 1855.

S. A. CLIFFORD.

S. A. Clifford was born in New Hampshire in 1814, and settled in Lynden in 1856. He opened up and cultivated a large farm in an intelligent manner, and made a success of farming. He was quite prominent in town and school affairs, holding offices in both town and school.

TNMAN PARCHER.

Tnman Parcher was born in Vermont, in 1811, and came to Lynden in 1857. He held the office of county commissioner and other important positions, but preferred a quiet life on his fine farm.

A C. POWERS.

Early in the spring of 1856, A. C. Powers, of Troy, New York, arrived in the town and took a claim. He returned to Troy in 1858 and came back to Minnesota in 1861. He was married in 1862 to Miss P. C. Heaton, at the residence of her father, T. Heaton. In 1864 he went back to New York and enlisted in a New York regiment and participated in several engagements. He served until the close of the war. In 1870 he bought a house and lot on the north side of the Clearwater river and has resided there ever since. He has held the responsible office of town clerk for about twenty years. His town record books are a model of neatness and good order. His family consisted of himself, wife and one daughter.

W. F. FISH.

W. F. Fish was born in Lunenburg, Vermont, in 1834. In 1857 he came to Minnesota and settled on the claim where he has lived ever since. He worked for government contractors hauling supplies for the Indians for some time. In February, 1865, he enlisted in the 1st Minnesota Heavy Artillery and was mustered out and discharged Oct. 9th at Fort Snelling. He returned to his farm, built a house and began life as a farmer. In 1867 he married Miss Sarah Townsand. For the last twenty years he has turned his attention to gardening and is considered the champion tomato and melon grower in central Minnesota.

W. T. RIGBY.

William Tuttle Rigby was born in the town of Oxford, Chenango County, N. Y., Sept. 14th, 1821. He was educated in the common schools and Academy of his native town, and did such mechanical, mercantile and common labor as circumstances brought to his hand.

He was married Dec. 11th, 1851, at Corning, N. Y., to Miss Mariette Rowley, who died Feby 18th, 1853. He was married again Nov. 1st, 1855, to Miss Susan Pearce and immigrated to Minneapolis the following May, and to the village of Clearwater in June, 1857. He commenced farming in 1859 on rented land. In 1864 he bought sixty-five acres of land in Lynden, in Dec. 20, and later purchased several other tracts, making a large and fine farm. He removed temporarily to the village of Clearwater in the spring of 1892, and in June 1895 adopted it as his permanent abode. The farm is now owned and occupied by his youngest son, C. T. Rigby. By his second marriage two sons and two daughters are living, the eldest, W. S. Rigby at Eau Claire Wis., the eldest daughter, Mavi E. married Col. S. B. McGuire, of Minneapolis, and the youngest daughter, Carrie M. married Charles Finch of Tioga Co., N. Y.

The subject of this sketch was elected a member of the Legislature for the year 1864, and re-elected for 1865, and has held the office of justice of the peace and member of the Board of Education for Clearwater graded school for twenty-four and twenty-one years respectively in succession, and is now the village postmaster.

CHARLES WHITEMORE.

Charles Whitemore was born in Dublin, New Hampshire, in 1812, and arrived in the town in May, 1861, and bought a farm and erected a house that fall. He was accompanied by his wife and eight children. He improved and beautified his farm by setting out trees and building good houses and barns until the place has become a well known land mark. He has been an extensive cattle feeder, shipping several car loads of fat cattle each spring. About sixteen years ago his sons, Joseph and Charles D. Whitemore, bought the farm from their father, and have since carried it on in the same intelligent manner.

JAMES COLGROVE.

James Colgrove was born in Hornellsville, N. Y., in 1841. He arrived in Lynden in 1866 and bought a large tract of land. He taught school for a number of years and then began improving and tilling his farm. His principal line in farming has been the feeding and fattening of cattle, shipping several car loads each year to eastern markets. His beautiful and highly cultivated farm indicates a practical and intelligent supervision. He has taken a deep interest in public affairs and has held prominent town and school officers most of the time since he became a resident of the town. He has invented and perfected a two horse potato digger that will undoubtedly revolutionize potato digging.

H. C. BARRETT.

Among the later arrivals in the town was H. C. Barrett, who was born in Battleborough, Vermont, in 1834. His occupation was farming and carpentering. He came to Clearwater in 1861, but in 1866 bough a farm in Lynden and moved onto it and cultivated it twenty-five years. He was justice of the perce and member of the school board for a long time.

History of Eden Lake.

By E. H. ATWOOD.

In writing up the early history of Eden Lake, as well as of many other towns, the historian has to depend largely upon the memory of the early settlers for the many facts and incidents necessarily required to faithfully portray the condition of the people and country in the pioneer days. Unfortunately the troublous times during the Sioux outbreak, and the anxious years of the Southern rebellion have tended to crowd out and nearly obliterate from memory the many exciting scenes and incidents that occurred prior to 1862. When one of the early pioneers is requested to recount some of the events that transpired in the early days of their settlement they have at first nothing to tell. The pages of memory of those days, so long ago, have grown dim. They have been laid away so long and have not been thought of for so many years that it needs something to bring them out; something to open up and bring out those dark pages of memory from their long slumber. A few questions skillfully put by the historian revives and brightens the memory and vividly recalls to mind the many scenes and incidents of their early days. They are thus enabled to recount the history of the early settlement of the town. They can tell of their privations and hardships, their struggles to overcome the many obstacles encountered in a new country without roads or bridges, without mills to grind their wheat or corn, and with no railroads within hundreds of miles, making it necessary to haul all of their supplies, except such as they raised on their farms, by teams a hundred miles over poor roads. Now they can remember and will tell of their primitive modes of farming, with poor plows and home made harrows, made with an ax, saw and suger. The harrow into which wooden teeth were inserted was hewn from a small tree. They cut their grain with a cradle, and their grass with a scythe, raking it by hand. Buggies and spring wagons were almost unknown. But wooden springs were hewed out and fastened in their lumber wagons and a board placed across them for a seat. Mr. A. Swisher recounts the manner of making roads in that early day. The residents were assessed four days poll tax which they worked out on the roads besides many days of volunteer work. For many years there were few, if any, legally laid out roads. The easiest route was selected for roads without regard to lines. If they could not pass around trees they cut them down low enough for a sled to pass over. If a road could not be made around a marsh or mud hole, a corduroy bridge was made by placing logs close together across the wet places and covered with a few brush and some earth. These roads were barely passable, and were very crooked, and as the land was bought up and improved, the owners objected having them meandering over their land, so they had to be changed and made over.

Mr. W. T. Mills tells of the long time it took him to cut or swamp a road to his claim. It took a strong wagon, a powerful team and slow and careful driving in those days to haul a load over these roads. The writer has a vivid recollection of a ride over these roads on a bob sled one winter with the Hon. D. J. Hanscom as driver and owner of the rig. We were in a hurry to get to the Grange meeting at the school house. The horses were not shod and the roads were icy and when the horses' feet came down upon the road they did not remain where they were placed but slid out in different directions, giving the horses the appearance of dancing a double schottische. While swiftly circling around one big tree and suddenly wheeling to the right to dodge another the runners of the bobsled would at the same time run up on the roots of still another, nearly pitching us out. However, running over a log on the other side would most likely right us up again. The Hon. gentleman did not seem to mind this rough riding. It must take several years' practice to become so used to such roads as to enjoy fast riding over them. But the same gentleman can now enjoy riding over fine roads through the town in a fine carriage behind a spirited horse. Everything comes to him who waits.

The following verse is taken from Eugene Field's description of the road to Bumpville, which fairly describes the roads in Eden Lake in its early days:

"Its bumpty bump and its jiggty jog,
    Journeying on to Bumpville.
It's over the hill tops and down through the bog,
    You ride on your way to Bumpville.
It's rattlety bang over boulder and stump;
    There are rivers to ford and fences to jump,
And the corduroy road it goes bumptybump,
    Mile after mile to Bumpville."

The town of Eden Lake is situated on the south line of Stearns county with the towns of Paynesville on the west and Lux-

emburg on the east. Nearly one-third of the northern part of the township is prairie while the rest of the town has been covered with a heavy growth of timber. In 1895 a large part of this timber had been cleared off and the land turned into beautiful farms with substantial houses and many large commodious barns and out buildings. The surface is undulating but the soil, especially in the southern two-thirds, is very fertile. It is believed that the soil of Eden Lake is the best adapted for dairy purposes of any town in the county. Its rich soil, its hills and valleys, its splendid natural meadows, its adaptability for the raising of all of the tame grasses, indicate that the town will in the near future become the leading dairy town of the county. Already many of the intelligent and progressive farmers of the town are gradually making preparations for a change from grain raising to dairy farming. Many believe that their soil is better adapted to clover and the tame grasses than it is to grain, although they raise large crops of all the different kinds of cereals. A creamery has been started in Eden Valley and is beginning to be well patronized. In anticipation of the change from grain farming to dairying, some farmers are gradually breeding into a class of cattle that are better adapted for milk and butter than those they now have.

What a contrast there is between the Eden Lake of to-day and that same territory thirty-five years ago. Now are found large cleared and well cultivated farms with fine buildings, and with pastures where large herds of cattle and other domestic animals graze in contentment. There are now fine, well-kept roads through the town. But go back thirty-five years. This township and the township of Munson formed one town. There was not a road in the township, and only two or three houses on the extreme north line. Two-thirds of the township was then an almost unbroken and uninhabited wilderness, and the first settlers found it a long and tedious undertaking to swamp a road through the wilderness of fallen timber and over wet marshes, so that they could get a team through with a load of household goods, and thus move their families to the places where they had located their claims.

There are several beautiful lakes in the town that are well supplied with several varieties of fish. The largest of these lakes is called Rice Lake. The others are Eden, Pitz, Brown, Vails and Long lakes. It is claimed that Charles Holifer was the first to settle in the town. He settled in the north part in 1856, and was followed that same year by Fred Herberger. The next year, B. Pirz and Ernst Holifer took claims in the northern part of the town. In 1858 Anton Huschle and Henry Boyer were among the arrivals. The next year John Meverle and Thomas Thomatz settled in the northern part of the town, and D. J. Hanscom, who was the first American to locate here, took the first claim in the southern portion. The next year Harley Clark took a claim adjoining Mr. Hanscom. He was accompanied by two sons and a daughter. John P. Meyer, Geo. Weis, Michael Weis and Mat Weis settle in the northern part of the town in 1860. There is no record of any more arrivals until 1863, when Harman Flint arrived. In 1864 Thomas A. Allyn and family, Geo. Nichols and A. Nichols arrived and took claims. In 1865 J. S. Reeves with his wife and three sons and one daughter, F. B. Smith, A. Swisher and family, Goin Hamilton, C. P. Russell, Wm. and Horace Vail, Adam Eppenberger and Morgan Driver came in and took claims. In 1866 the following were among the new arrivals: P. Vanblarigan, Wm. Marquett, Silas Cos-airt, James Jones, W. T. Mills, R. McGuire, Rev. Wilkins. In 1867 L. S. Bennett arrived and took a claim and W. R. Hoskins came in 1868.

The territory comprising the town of Eden Lake was a part of the disputed hunting ground between the great Sioux nation of Indians and the Chippewas. The Sioux claimed the territory as exclusively their own for hunting purposes, as far north as several miles north of St. Cloud. But the Chippewas often ventured upon this ground to hunt and often lost scalps by their temerity.

In the spring of 1857 a party of six Chippewas were hunting in the vicinity of Rice Lake and had their camp near the shore. The Sioux soon discovered them and succeeded in killing and scalping one of the Chippewas and capturing their camp. The other five fled and escaped. That fall eight Chippewas came there to hunt. Samuel Wakefield had a small shanty without any floor but the ground. B Pirz had his shanty about one mile from Wakefield's. These Indians came to Wakefield's shanty to sleep at night. It is a custom among the Germans to fire off guns Christmas eve and New Years at midnight. B. Pirz had an old fashioned six shooter and concluded to inaugurate the old country custom in his new home, so at midnight he fired off the six shots. The Chippewas were sleeping on the floor of Wakefield's shanty. They heard the shots and sprang to their feet shouting "Sioux! Sioux!" and grabbing their guns bounded out into the darkness, and such was their fearful dread of their enemy that they never stopped their wild flight until they were safe in their own country. Up to the year 1864 there were only a few settlers on the north line of the town, and two or three in the southern part.

In 1862, at the beginning of the Sioux outbreak, Harley Clark's was the only family in the south part of the town. He took his family to Maine Prairie and then to Minneapolis and remained away until fall. There were about six German families in the north part of the town that remained at home for some time, but when Paynesville was attacked they fled to Mr. Middendorf's house near Richmond. On the second night, towards morning some Indians fired at the house.

The shot could be heard rattling against the building. The me inside made a great noise and the Indians were frightened and ran away.

In 1863, although the Indians committed no depredations in the town, it was known that small parties of Sioux were in the neighboring towns and that they might make a raid into their town at any time. So the people were kept in a state of uneasiness during a large part of that summer.

In the latter part of the year 1866 the inhabitants of the township which is now Eden Lake, but which then was a part of the town of Munson, believing that there were enough inhabitants in their township to organize a separate town, obtained the necessary authority from the Board of County Commissioners to meet and organize by electing the necessary town officers. Accordingly they held a special meeting for that purpose. The following is taken from the first town records:

"Minutes of special town meeting held Feb. 16th, 1867, for the purpose of organizing the town of Eden Lake, Stearns county, Minn. Harley Clark was chosen clerk, T. R. McGuire, Moderator. W. T. Mills, J. Farrer and James Jones were chosen judges of election. The following officers were elected: Supervisors: W. T. Mills, Chairman, and T. R. McGuire and Earnest Holifer. Clerk, D. J. Hanscom; Assessor, C. P. Russell; Treasurer, Thomas A. Allyn; Justice of the Peace, James Jones and B. Pirz; Constables, Goin Hamilton and Wm. Marquett.

HARLEY CLARK, clerk of the meeting.

"Minutes of the first annual Town meeting held in Eden Lake, at the house of Wm. Marquet, on Tuesday the 7th day of April, 1867. C. P. Russell was elected and sworn in as moderator. Horace Vail was appointed and sworn in as judge of the town meeting to fill a vacancy. The electors voted to raise a tax of three mills on the dollar for town revenue. The following persons were elected to office. Supervisors, W. T. Mills, chairman; T.

R. McGuire and Earnest Holifer; D. J. Hanscom, clerk; C. P. Russell, assessor; W. T. Mills and B. Pirz, justices of the peace; Wm. Marquett and Ernst Holifer, constables; Goin Hamilton, treasurer. The vote for division of the town, 13. Against division of the town, 24.

D. J HANSCOM, Town Clerk.

At a meeting of the su ervisors April 23rd, 1867, four days poll tax was assessed to each man liable to do highway labor.

At the second annual town meeting held April 7th, 1868, the following by-laws were passed.

"That all cattle, sheep, hogs, asses and horses shall be allowed to run at large between the first day of April and the 15th day of October of each year. That a fence to be lawful shall be six rails high and a rider, or eight rails high, the rails to be four inches apart.

D. J. HANSCOM, Town Clerk."

Many of the church and school records prior to 1864 are either lost or were not kept as they can be found only in the memory of the early settlers, and as these people are aged, it will not be long before they will have passed away and these valuable records will be lost to the world, unless secured soon.

EDEN LAKE SCHOOL DISTRICT.

The first school district in Eden Lake was No. 19. It was organized in 1865. The first officers were: John Leindecker, director; Charles Holifer, treasurer; B. Pirz, clerk. The first teacher was B. Pirz in 1865, and the second teacher was Tobias Sleeper in 1866. The school house was built in 1865. The territory comprising this district included all of the present town of Eden Lake and one tier of sections on the south side of Munson.

SCHOOL DISTRICT 68.

This district was organized in 1869, and the school house was built the next year. The first officers elected were: C. P. Russell, clerk; W. T. Mills, director; D. J. Hanscom, treasurer

Miss Lizzie Abbott taught the first school in 1870, beginning July 25th. Mrs. Margaret Wynings taught the same school the next winter Mrs. D. J. Hascom, who was Miss Lizzie Abbott before marriage, taught the 3d term in the winter of 1871-2.

SCHOOL DISTRICT NO. 69.

School District No. 69 was organized about the year 1870 and its first officers were John Cornairt, Silas Cornairt and James Jones. Miss Cordelia Day, of Maine Prairie, taught the first school in 1871, and Mrs. Wynings taught the two next terms. Miss Mary Greely, (now Mrs. W. F. Street,) of Maine Prairie, taught the school in 1876. The officers then were A. Swisher, treasurer; Noah Wiles, director; John Welliver, clerk; Mrs. Street gives a very interesting account of the condition of the town at that time. She says that Mr. Welliver, the Clerk, told her that she looked too young to teach such a large school, but handed her a slate and pencil and said if you will draw a township plat and put in all the sections numbered correctly, you can have the school. It took her but a few minutes to properly draw the township and thus secured the school. She taught this school two terms. There was no store nearer than Mannannah, and the nearest railroad was at Litchfield. They had a weekly mail. Mr Reeves was postmaster, and William Hoskins carried the mail from Cold Spring. Elder Shoemaker, of Maine Prairie, came out occasionally to preach.

SCHOOL DISTRICT NO. 77.

This district was organized in 1884, and at its first school meeting in July, 1885, the following officers were elected Mich. O'Brien, director; John W Driver, treasurer; Curtis Robbins, clerk. The school house was built that year and Miss Ada Dye taught the two first terms. Hattie Rogers was the next teacher

EDEN LAKE CHURCHES.

In 1875 Rev C. Scott organized an association called the Church of God. Their first minister was Rev. S. P. Matheny, who officiated two years and was followed by Revs. Jnd. Raymond, Wm. Parsons, O. R Jenks and E. E. Torma. The church

building was erected in 1892, but is not yet completed or dedicated. They held their meetings in private houses and school houses until the church was built. The first officers were, Elders, W. T. Mills and D. J. Hanscom. The first deacons were Morgan Driver and H. W. Welliver. There are now, in 1895, about one hundred members in good standing belonging to this church.

CHRISTIAN CHURCH.

The first Christian church of Eden Lake was organized in 1869 by the Rev. Wm. Cameron. They had no church building, but held their meetings in private houses and had for some time quite a flourishing organization, but for many causes the organization was discontinued, and in 1887 the present Christian church organization was completed and a church building erected in the village of Eden Valley just over the line in Meeker county. The first trustees were J. H. Reeves, F. B. Smith, Ursom White, S. Cornairt, J. G. Reeves and J. S. Reeves. The first elders were L. Rails and Ursom White. The first deacons were F. B. Smith and J. H. Reeves. Rev. John Truax was their first minis er, followed by W. W. Pew and at present Rev. J. A. Grice is officiating.

CATHOLIC CHURCH.

In 1894 the Catholic church of Eden Valley was organized and their church building built and finished at a cost of about $10,000. About seventy-five families attend the church. The first officers when organized were three trustees named M. E. Weiler, Jacob Hammes and Peter Hanson. The church was incorporated in 1895. Its present laymen are Jacob Hammes and Peter Hanson.

EDEN LAKE PATRONS OF HUSBANDRY.

In 1874 a Grange of the Patrons of Husbandry was organized with D J. Hanscom, master; Elihu Swisher, treasurer; and John Willohy, secretary. This was an organization of farmers and their wives and sons and daughters. This society was kept up for a number of years. The meetings of the Grange were pleasant and

beneficial to its members in many ways.
It promoted social intercourse and benefit-
ed them financially and intellectually and
the old members regret that it was allowed
to die out.

LITERARY SOCIETIES.

During the long winter months in the
new settlement, literary societies were
formed. These organizations were rather
primitive. But at stated intervals they
would have some literary entertainment,
such as debates, essays, recitations, &c.
These were kept up for many years.

This ends the early history of Eden
Lake. The writer tenders his thanks to
the many citizens of that town who have
assisted in this work.

The following brief biographical sketches
all refer to the pioneers of Eden Lake:

BARTHOLOME PERZ.

B. Perz was one of the first to settle in
the northern part of Eden Lake. He has
been closely identified with all of the town
affairs. He was born in Austria in 1819.
His occupation, after he had finished his
education, was bookkeeper in government
position. He came to Minnesota in 1854
and settled at Sauk Rapids. The next
year he went to Cold Spring, where he remained two years and then took a claim
in Eden Lake. The next year he married
Miss Johanna Holiter, and then settled on
his claim and began improving it. In
1860 he went to Pike's Peak and New
Mexico and engaged in mining for three
years. He then returned and bought his
present farm in sections 5 and 6. He was
appointed superintendent of common
schools to fill a vacancy, caused by the
death of the superintendent, Dr. Tolman.
He represented his district in the legislature two terms, from 1873 to 1875, and
with the exception of five years he has
been county commissioner from 1866 to
1896, as well as a member of the town and
school boards. He taught the first school
in his school district in 1865. His children are Josephine, Magdaline, Joseph,
Angeline and John.

D. J. HANSCOM.

The history of Eden Lake would be incomplete without the mention of D. J.
Hanscom, who has been closely identified
with the town since its earliest settlement.
Mr Hanscom was born in York county,
Maine, Aug. 23d, 1833. He engaged in
agricultural pursuits until he was 19 years
of age, when he engaged for three years
in the mercantile business. In 1856 he
come to Wisconsin, and the next year to
St. Paul and engaged in the lumber business until 1859, when he located a claim
in Eden Like, being the first American
settler in the town. In 1861 he enlisted
in Company D, 4th regiment, and remained with the regiment until 1864, when
he was honorably discharged. Returning
to Eden Lake he took the homestead on
which he still resides He was the first
town clerk in the town and retained that
office for ten years He was also assessor
for 8 years supervisor 14 years, and treasurer 15 years. Besides this he has been
on the school board 25 years. He represented his district in the legislature in
1881. Mr. Hanscom and Miss Lizzie
Abbott were married Feb. 22d 1871. Their
children's names are Geo., E. Stella L.
and Ella S.

FRANK B. SMITH

Frank B. Smith, although one of the
later arrivals in town, has been very prominent in all town affairs. He was born in
Vermillion county, Illinois, in 1849, and
grew up to manhood on a farm. In 1865
he came to Minnesota, but returned after
a two years sojourn. In 1875 he again
sought the fertile lands of Eden Lake and
bought and improved a farm, and in 1881
Mr. Smith and Miss Julia E. Maxwell
were married. They now have two children. Mr. Smith has held responsible offices in town and school boards almost
since residence in the town. He was town
clerk three years, assessor eleven years,
supervisor one year and was a member of
the school board many years and at present is president of the village council of
Eden Lake. He was a prominent mem-

her of the Patrons of Husbandry. When he bought his farm it was in the wilds of Eden Valley with roads so bad they were traveled with difficulty. Now this same farm is a part of the flourishing village of Eden Valley and many trains pass in sight of his house on the " oo." railroad.

A. SWISHER.

A Swisher was born in Vermillion county, Illinois, in 1821, and was brought up as a farmer. In 1865 he came to Eden Lake and bought a farm and improved it, and has remained on it ever since. The village of Eden Lake has absorbed his land and he is now a resident of that village although living in the same house that he built in 1867 when there were no roads fit to be called by that name in the town.

SILAS COSSAIRT

Silas Cossairt was born in Vermillion county, Illinois, in 1837. Farming was his principal occupation. In 1865 he moved to Maine Prairie, Minn , and to Eden Lake the next year. He took a claim of 160 acres and bought 80 acres more. He has improved and operated his farm ever since. He married Alvira Swisher in 1860 and had three children when he arrived in the town viz: Mary B., Samuel and Geo. D. Mr. Cossairt has been quite a traveler. He has been a member of the town and school board many years and is now a member of the council of Eden Valley.

The following brief biographical sketches all refer to the pioneers of Eden Lake:

GOIN HAMILTON.

In 1865 Goin Hamilton arrived in Eden Lake and entered 160 acres of land, which he improved, but sold that and bought his present farm, where he still resides. Mr. Hamilton's life has been an active one and he has seen much of the world as a citizen and as a soldier. He was born in the north of Ireland in 1825. The business of his younger days was a bleacher of linen. He came to New York in 1845 and worked in several states, but when the

Mexican war broke out he enlisted in the regular army, and served in Mexico and on the Pacific coast. After his time expired in the army he worked in the gold mines of California for a number of years. He enlisted and served two years in the rebellion and re-enlisted as a veteran. After his checkered career he settled down and is operating his farm in an intelligent manner.

MORGAN DRIVER.

Morgan Driver was born in Randolph county, Indiana, in 1828, and was brought up on a farm. He has worked occasionally at shoemaking, but farming has been his principal occupation. In 1862 he enlisted in an Indiana regiment, served until the close of the war, and was discharged in 1865. He came to Eden Lake the same year. Mr. Driver and Miss Mary A. Hedrich were married in 1856. When they arrived at Eden Lake in 1865 they were accompanied by their two sons, John W. and Morgan F., and their daughter Mary A These children are all married now. Mr. Driver took a homestead in 1865 and still lives upon it. Mr. Driver preferred to live a quiet life but consented to act on the school board.

L. S. BENNETT.

L. S. Bennett was born in Ohio in 1833 and came to Minnesota in 1856 and settled in ! e Sueur county, but in 1867 he and his wife came to Eden Lake and took a claim which he improved and operated until his death in 1893. His children, Angelette, Delila, Charles, Nancy, Alfred, Matilda and Angeline, accompanied them to this place. All of these children except Matilda, who is dead, are alive and married. Mrs. Bennett's maiden name was Miss Elizabeth Woodfield.

J. S. REEVES.

J. S. Reeves was born in Ohio in 1832. When quite a small boy he moved with his parents to Indiana. Mr. Reeves and Miss Martha J. Campbell were married in 1853. He came to Minnesota in 1862 and settled in Omstead county. That fall he enlisted in Brackett's Battalion and

served on the f ontier until 1865 He
came to Stearns county in the fall of 1865
and settled in Eden Lake. His three sons,
J. H., J. G. and Wm. M., and his
daughter, Anna J, accompanied him.
They are all now (in 1895) living at or
near Eden Valley. J. H. is a grain buyer
at Eden Valley. J. G. has charge of the
grain elevator at Kimball. Wm. M. is
taking a four year's course at the North
Western Christian College. Anna J.
married Mr. Wm. Workman.

W. T. MILLS.

W. T. Mills has been quite prominent
in the affairs of Eden Lake. He was born
in Randolph county, Indiana, in 1834, and
has been a farmer all his life, except three
years, in which he engaged in the dry
goods business. In 1866 he came to Eden
Lake with his wife and two sons, Wm. R.
and Noah , and daughter, Abigal J.
The two sons are married and living on
farms near the homestead. Mr. Mills has
held the office of chairman of supervisors
nearly ever since he came here, being the
first chairman of the town. He has also
been a member of the school board twenty-
five years. He has followed an intelligent

plan of diversified farming, which has been
quite successful.

W. R. HOSKINS

W. R. Hoskins was born in Vermillion
county, Illinois, in 1831, his parents being
farmers. He came from there to Eden
Lake in 1868 and took a claim of 160 acres,
which he has improved and operated ever
since. His principal line in farming was
raising cattle and horses as well as grain.
He has been a member of the school board
for many years. His farm shows careful
and intelligent cultivation.

JAMES JONES.

James Jones, one of Eden Lake's progressive farmers, was born in Randolph
county, Indiana, in 1838. He enlisted in
the army in 1864 and served two years
and three months, and was mustered out
in 1866. He then came to Eden Lake,
taking a homestead of 160 acres and buying 20 acres more. He has improved this
farm and raised large numbers of horses
and cattle, besides hay and grain. He was
one of the first justices of the peace in the
town and has been a member of the town
and school boards.

History of Paynesville.

By E. H. ATWOOD.

The town of Paynesville is situated in the southwestern part of Stearns county. Near the center of the town is the present incorported village of Paynesville. The surface of the town is rather level prairie in the northern part, while the southern part is undulating and prior to settlement was covered with brush and timber. The northwestern part is rolling prairie. The soil varies from a light sandy to a dark rich loam, with a clay subsoil, and is very fertile. The North Fork of the Crow River enters the town in section 18, and flows in an easterly and southerly direction, entering Lake Koronis in section 35. This lake is quite large with several beautiful islands. It lies in the southern part of the town and extends into Meeker county. It is a picturesque lake with its islands, its many bays and indentations, its bold wooded promontories and low grassy nooks, and ever changing panorama of shore and islands which it presents to those coasting around it. Its beauties together with the invigorating and health-giving atmosphere which obtains in this region cannot fail to make Lake Koronis one of the famous and ideal watering places and healthful resorts in Minnesota.

Tradition says that the honor of making the first claims in the town belong to Messrs. McCormach and Bullard. They located the first townsite in Paynesville in 1856; but when the town was surveyed and subdivided in the following spring it was found that they had located on section sixteen, and this being a school section, could not be taken as a townsite and so of course had to be abandoned. The honor of making the first permanent claim in the town belongs to Edwin E. Payne who settled on section seventeen but a short distance from where McCormach and Bullard had located their claim.

During the summer of 1857 a postoffice was established in the village and E. E. Payne was appointed postmaster. The mail was carried by Mr. Evans on foot from Traver-de-Sioux to St. Cloud via Paynesville once a week.

Mr. Payne was followed the same summer, 1857, by J. E. Pease, Geo. Lincoln, W. P. Bennett, Richard Porter, Dwight Twitchel, T. C. McClure, J. H. Boylan, John Boylan, August Smith, John Baitenger, and Fred Herberger. The two latter settled in the eastern part of the town; the others at or near the village. Elder C. S. Harrison, a Congregational minister, began preaching at Paynesville this year, being the first minister in the place. He held his meetings in private houses until a school house was built several years later. That fall Grace Lincoln was gladly welcomed as the first child born in the new settlement.

The townsite of Paynesville was located

by E. E. Payne in 1857. Soon after a townsite company was organized, consisting of T. C. McClure, H. C. Waite, E. E. Payne, O. S. Freeman and Mr. Parks. The townsite was surveyed and platted that summer by E. E. Payne. O. S. Freeman, W. P. Bennett and D. Twitchel erected houses on it that summer. The townsite company failed to fulfill their part of the proceedings necessary to hold it as a townsite and the land was sold at the government land sale in October, 1860. It was bid in by Robert Blakely who soon after deeded it to Waite and McClure. The original townsite was then vacated, and in 1861 about one-half of the original was surveyed and platted by John Blakely.

Among the new arrivals in 1858 were Hugh Blakely, John Blakely, N. M. Freeman, Stephen Harris, Luther Brown, Christopher Wessel and Christian Rien. Later arrivals were Gottlieb Knebel, Michael Schultz, August Knebel and Andrew Eckemeir.

Among the arrivals in 1859 was Daniel Chisholm.

During the winter of 1859-60 the settlers had somewhat improved their conditions. Such food as they could raise was abundant, but the cost of hauling goods by team from St. Anthony made it difficult to obtain them. Therefore nearly all luxuries of the table were dispensed with. In March of 1860 occurred the first death in the new settlement, that of Luther Brown. The community was small in numbers and his loss was deeply felt by all.

Among the arrivals in the new settlement in 1860 were Christ. Helmer, Fred Schroeder, Anton Wartenberg, Fred Gedosch, Wilhelm Helmer, George W. Prior, S. P. Roach and Lyman Reed.

In 1861 Edward H. Bates settled in the town and opened the first blacksmith shop. This was greatly needed in this far off frontier town.

The first crop of grain that amounted to much was grown in 1860, and that fall and early winter the first threshing machine ever operated in the town was owned and run by Wm. Maybee and his brother-in-law, Mr. Wm. Lee. Mr. Maybee was afterwards killed by the Indians at Mannanah in 1862. The settlers were obliged to haul their grain to St. Cloud, a distance of thirty-three to forty miles, and had to go to the same place for their dry goods and groceries. Until 1861 the nearest blacksmith shop was at Jacob's Prairie, a distance of over twenty miles, and the nearest store was at St. Joe, twenty-six miles away.

In the early days the merchants exchanged their goods for eggs and butter, which they sent to St. Paul. For a number of years there was quite a demand for some wheat and a large quantity of oats at Cold Spring to supply the new settlers on the Red River and other localities to the west, until they could raise them themselves. During the Indian war in 1862 to 1864, there was a good market at home for oats, at fair prices, to feed the government horses, stationed at different frontier towns. Then in 1864 there was a rush of immigrants to the Red River and the counties west of Stearns. Their needs furnished a good market for all kinds of produce.

The Paynesville people found a good sale for their produce at Sauk Centre, from whence it was shipped to the new settlements.

When the railroad was built to the south they hauled their produce there. In the early days when the people generally used oxen, it took three to four days to go to St. Cloud. In summer they camped out while on these journeys, sleeping under the wagon. These trips were quite notable events. When anyone intended to make the journey it would be known several days beforehand, and many of their neighbors would send by them for things they needed. One would want to send eggs to be exchanged for groceries, others wanted dry goods and all sorts of things, so that the departure or return of a settler from one of these trips was quite an important matter. It is claimed that the people in those days were more neighborly, hospitable and generous. There was no stealing and but very little quarreling.

The people were happy and cheerful and looked hopefully forward for a brighter future.

The spring of 1861 found the condition of the pioneers in and around Paynesville somewhat improved, after four long years of the hardships and privations that usually befall the first settlers on the frontier of a new country. So far it had been a long, hard struggle to subdue the wild land and bring it into a condition to yield the bountiful crops of which its fertile soil was capable. This patriotic town was in a poor condition to properly respond to the first calls for volunteers in the spring of 1861. All who could be spared enlisted and went to the front. But the situation of many was such that it seemed impossible to go and leave their families on the exposed frontier, so poorly prepared to take care of themselves. Besides, in the years 1862 and 1863 these settlers had their hands full in protecting their homes and families from the savage foes that ravaged and desolated the surrounding country. But, after the danger from the Indian depre'ations were over, and before the close of the war, this town nobly furnished her quota of volunteers.

In July of 1862, T. H. Barrett, of St. Cloud, came to Paynesville and called a mass meeting at the school house, made a patriotic speech and was followed by N Darnell. As a result of the meeting M. P Beckley, P Luce and W. N. Darnell enlisted in Captain Asa Libby's company, 7th regiment, and Alfred Harris and G. W. Reed enlisted in T. H. Barrett's company, 9th regiment. Another mass meeting was called in March, 1865, to see if enough would enlist to clear the town from the impending draft. As a result of this meeting John Phipps, William Blakely, Daniel Chisholm, John J. Brown,

Evan Thomas. W. P. Bennett and H. Jones enlisted in the 1st regiment.

The following is taken from the St. Cloud Democrat of March 2d, 1865:

"Plucky Town: The town of Paynesville with twenty-seven men enrolled has a quota of nine. One of this number enlisted some time ago, and yesterday eight of the best citizens of the town, under the leadership of Postmaster Phipps, arrived in this city on their way to St. Paul to clear Paynesville of the draft by going in themselves."

The three following brave sons of Paynesville were offered up as a sacrifice to the cause of human freedom while in the army:

William Beckley died at St. Peter, this state, in December, 1862, of measles.

William Blakely died in hospital at City Point, May 6th, 1865

Geo. W. Reed died at St. Louis, Mo., Oct. 20, 1864

The following are among those that enlisted from the town of Paynesville and served in the army during the Rebellion:

In the First Minnesota Regiment were: John Phipps, William Blakely, Daniel Chisholm, John J. Brown, Evan Thomas, W. P. Bennett and H. Jones. Third Minnesota Regiment, S. P. Roach. Fourth Minnesota Regiment, Andrew Eichemeir and William Helmer. Seventh Minnesota Regiment, Michael P. Beckley, W. N. Darnell and Harrison P. Luce. Eighth Minnesota Regiment, Joseph J. Reed. Ninth Minnesota Regiment, Alfred Harris, Geo. W. Reed. First Regiment Heavy Artillery, John Blakely. Hatch's Battalion, Smith Flanders. Mounted Rangers, Robert and John Blakely, John J. Brown, Anton Wartenburg, August Schultz and Wm. Schroeder. Second Cavalry, Stephen F. Brown and Smith Flanders. First Regiment of Mounted Volunteers, Wm. Beckley.

The inhabitants of Paynesville were very busy securing their crops of grain and hay in August, 1862. About the 20th of August, the first news of the Sioux outbreak reached the village. The day previous, a wedding had been in progress at the upper end of Norway lake, and the ceremony was just about to be performed when a little boy came rushing into their midst with the startling intelligence that the Indians had killed his brother and sister. All was confusion in the little household and the party broke up, and the guests at the wedding immediately started for their homes. They soon met a party of Indians who acted very kindly, shaking hands all around, and appearing pleased to meet them. But, watching their opportunity, they began shooting the whites, killing all but Mrs. Lunegburg, who at the first hostile movement of the Indians, sprang into a small stream surrounded by tall reeds and sank into the water up to her mouth. She there witnessed the savages torture her companions in the most fiendish and horrible manner that their ingenerity could invent. They cut off a little baby's fingers one by one and then its ears and nose, finding pleasure in seeing the child squirm and scream. They protracted the torture of their victims as long as possible and until death ended their sufferings. After all were dead and it had grown dark, Mrs. Lunegburg started for assistance, reaching the house of Ole Gergonson about three o'clock in the morning and aroused them from their slumber. She had traveled about eight miles straight north over a very rough country. Early the next morning they all came to Paynesville and reported the massacre. This was the first news received at Paynesville of the outbreak. Preparations for the defense of the settlers were immediately begun. A party consisting of John and Hugh Blakely, Moses Pelkey, Stephen Harris, Smith Flander, Hugh Jones, John Johnson and others at once started for the scene of the massacre. Arriving there about five o'clock p. m., they found thirteen dead bodies close together and two others near by. They buried them all in one grave. They then went into camp. The next morning they discovered

that a party of Indians had camped on the other side of a ridge that night, neither party aware of the presence of the other. They then started for the settlement at the east end of the lake. They soon heard firing, and hastening forward found the Indians attacking this settlement. They rushed to the assistance of the whites, causing the savages to beat a hasty retreat to the timber three miles away. The settlers then hastily loaded up their goods and families into wagons and collected such stock as they could and started for Paynesville, where they arrived that night escorted by the Paynesville party. Soon refugees from the south and west began pouring into the town. That night a meeting was called and a company of home guards organized. Stephen Harris was chosen captain, John Blakely first lieutenant and Hugh Blakely second lieutenant and John J. Brown sergeant. There were about thirty men in the settlement. It was voted to build a sod fort forty-one hundred feet square. That night guards were detailed to keep watch and all possible precautions taken for safety. There was but little sleep that night, for it was feared that their exposed settlement would be attacked before morning.

Early the next morning the men went to work on their sod fort. They expected the Indians to soon attack them and worked with all possible haste to get a place of safety for the women and children. The church and school buildings were hauled up to make two corners of the fort, while two dwelling houses occupied the other corners. A wall of sods four feet thick was to be so built as to enclose these buildings with bastians at the corners. Scouts were kept out on the watch to prevent a surprise, and at night the women and children occupied the fort and the men took turns guarding the outside. Pickets were sent out about 80 rods on the different sides, to give timely warning of the approach of any foe.

The men inside the fort slept with their

arms at their sides, ready at a moment's warning, in case of need. In two or three days they had the sides of the fort built up five feet high, with provisions and water and preparations to sink a well for water if needed They felt that now they could stand quite a siege.

About this time a company of volunteers from St. Cloud, under Captain Ambrose Freeman, came up and scoured the country to the south and west to assist any who might be found in danger on the frontier, and to bury the dead. After two days they returned to Paynesville. They remained all night at that place and the next morning returned to St. Cloud, accompanied by most of the refugees who had fled from homes on the frontiers and also many inhabitants of Paynesville. This so weakened the garrison at the fort that it was deemed unsafe and unwise to remain any longer, for news reached them daily of terrible fighting and horrible atrocities committed by the Indians. The fort was consequently abandoned and all went to Richmond or other places for safety. For a short time Paynesville was entirely abandoned, but after remaining away a week or so many returned to the village. But soon the news came that a large force of Indians were coming that way. The settlers had but little ammunition, they were few in numbers, their fort was insufficient, and it was deemed unsafe to stay so they again left Paynesville for a safer place farther east Some stopped at Richmond and some at St. Cloud and other places.

Several days passed and no fresh news of Indian depredations were heard of in the direction of Paynesville. The citizens had left in haste and their grain was mostly in the shock and none threshed out. They were in great need of food for themselves and such stock as they had been able to secure. This was about the 11th of September, when nine brave, resolute men determined to secure some of the grain.

They went back to their homes with several teams and a threshing machine outfit. At night they slept in the school house in the sod fort and placed their teams and cattle in the fort. They had been threshing during the day and on the night of the 13th returned to the fort, greatly fatigued with their day's labor. After securing their teams and cattle inside the fort and partaking of a hasty supper, they lay down in the school house to sleep, leaving their dog on the front steps for a sentinel. Not a sign of an Indian had so far been seen and nothing had been disturbed since they had left their homes the week before. So they deemed it safe for all to sleep. While soundly sleeping they were rudely awakened. A bright light was shining into the school house from the burning church and from the school house. Mr. John Boylan stepped to the door to ascertain the cause and was shot by an Indian inside the fort and severely wounded. This convinced those inside the school house that they were being attacked by the Indians. Mr. Boylan dropped down and crawled under a wagon where it was so dark that the Indians could not see him. Watching his opportunity he made his way back into the house. From what they heard and saw they were convinced that the Indians did not know 'where the whites were. They could see the Indians in the fort, the bright light revealing them very plainly, and they could have shot a number of them. But as they were outnumbered and knew that if they did shoot it would disclose their whereabouts to the Indians and endanger their own lives, they refrained from shooting. Finding that the Indian guards on the outside had come into the fort to assist in securing the horses, they quietly scaled the walls and, keeping in the shadow of the building as much as possible, they started for the river bank, (Crow River,) about one hundred rods distant. Part of the way over which they had to pass was lighted up as bright as day from the burning church. The Indians caught sight of them while in this lighted space and poured a volley of shot after them, fortunately without doing any harm, and they succeeded in reaching the wooded bank of the river. John and Robert Blakely remained with the wounded man, carrying him nearly three miles in the dark, and finally reached a deserted house. Here they found a cotton shirt with which they bound up the wound. Mr. Boylan was nearly dead from loss of blood, the ball passing within one-fourth of an inch of an artery. The few settlers in the eastern part of the town were warned of their danger and hastened to Richmond. A party from that place came out the next morning and brought the wounded man in and held the Indians in check until all the settlers had reached Richmond. The names of the nine men in the fort were John, Hugh and Robert Blakely, O. S. Freeman, Hugh Jones, Smith Flanders, E. H. Bates, Peter Lagrow and John Boylan. The Indians succeeded in taking off some ten or twelve horses, some oxen and cows and considerable other plunder.

After the attack on the fort and the burning of buildings in the fort, and nearly all of the buildings in the village, the citizens remained away until about the 20th of October. At this time the government sent Company E and *H, of the Twenty-fifth Wisconsin Regiment, to Paynesville. They immediately began to enlarge and strengthen the fort and to take measures to secure the safety of the settlers. A large number of the settlers then returned to their homes, some finding only a heap of ruins, others finding their homes despoiled of everything of value. The troops remained until the middle of December, when they were sent south, and their places were taken by Company A, of the Mounted Rangers. This company remained during the winter.

While these conflicts with the Indians were taking place in the village of Paynesville, a little settlement of Germans on the eastern side of the town were also having their troubles. At the first alarm about ten families gathered at the house of Gottlob Knebel, and all united in building a sod breast work around the house. They remained there two weeks, the women and children remaining in the house thus fortified, and the men to the number of fifteen would go out together to secure their crops, first on one farm and then on another, always keeping someone on guard and keeping near their guns. After about two weeks, concluding that danger was over, most of them returned to their own homes. That very night the Indians attacked and burned the fort at Paynesville, and early in the morning the settlers were warned of their danger and all hastened to Richmond. During their stay in their little fort, guards had been kept out and relieved every two hours, and every precaution taken to guard against a surprise. On the second night after they arrived in Richmond the house they were in was fired upon by Indians. The next morning a party persued these Indians for a long distance, the Indians burning houses, barns and hay stacks as they went along.

In the fall of 1862 Waite and McClure opened a small store.

In the spring of 1863 most of the inhabitants of Paynesville returned to their homes, but on the big prairies to the south and west, few dared to return to the homes from which they had been driven the fall before. As early as May rumors of Indian depredations reached the village. May 2d three soldiers of the 8th regiment were shot by the Indians near Pomme De Terre. In June Captain Cady and three men of Company A followed the trail of Indians near Kandiyohi Lake, where they overtook and opened fire upon them. The Indians returned the fire and Captain Cady was shot through the heart, and the Indians escaped. A detachment of Company E followed a trail of Indians in Wright county and exchanged shots with them, but they also escaped. A sad event, which cast a deep gloom over the community of Paynesville, occurred on the 11th of

September. On the morning of that day Captain Rutherford, Seargent Edwards and another man of Company A, left Paynesville for Maanannh, taking the place for the day of the regular patrol of Company E on that road. When only a short distance out, they were fired upon by Indians in ambush, who were evidently waiting for the patrol. Seargent Edwards was shot and fell from his horse. Captain Rutherford received a bullet through his clothes and returned to Paynesville. All of Company E who had horses immediately started in pursuit. They found Seargent Edwards scalped and dead. They followed the trail of the Indians until it was lost near Green Lake. The soldiers remained at Paynesville until May 24, 1864.

In 1865 Josiah Waite opened a store. He sold out his store in 1867 to Darby & Moore.

The first mill was a steam saw mill built on Lake Koronia by Egbert Ostrander and Lyman Chandler, in 1868 and the next year they built a flouring mill on the north side of Crow River, in the village. This mill was afterwards moved to the south side.

Among the arrivals in 1866 were James C. Haines, who was a native of Canada. He held the office of justice of the peace for a number of years, as well as other town and school offices and was appointed postmaster. Egbert Ostrander also arrived this year from New York. He kept a hotel for many years in Paynesville.

PAYNESVILLE SCHOOLS.

The Baitenger school district, No. 43, was organized in 1868 and the first school meeting was held in March of that year. Its first officers were elected as follows: John Schoenleben, director; Andrew Eckmire, clerk; John Baitenger, treasurer. Emma Elliot was the first teacher after the organization and she was followed by W. P. Bennett. Their present school house was built in 1868 Mary Blakely taught school in John Baitenger's house in 1867.

SCHOOL DISTRICT NO. 52.

The first officers of this district were Dwight Twichell, director; Hugb Blakely, clerk; Jacob Staples, treasurer. The first teacher was Mrs. Alsina Blakely,who taught 3 months in 1867. Mrs. J. W. Sivers taught three months in 1868. The schools were taught in a grainery until 1872, when the present house was built.

SCHOOL DISTRICT NO. 162.

School district No. 162 was organized in 1892. Its first officers were Henry Block, director; Homer Beckley, treasurer; Charles Hudson, Clerk. Their house was built that year. Ida A. Brown was the first teacher. She was succeeded by Dallie Young.

SCHOOL DISTRICT NO. 27.

From the best accounts obtainable the first school organized in the town of Paynesville was situated in the village. A frame school house was built in the spring of 1862 and Miss F. Reed taught a six weeks term that summer. This house was one of four afterwards enclosed in the sod fort and was burned by the Indians in September of that year. In the fall of 1863 the house was rebuilt with logs and Robt. Hoover taught the school that winter. Mrs W. P. Bennett, S. P. Roach and Mrs Daniel Chisholm are authorities for these statements. A log school house had been commenced in the spring of 1859, but the terrible storm of May 31st blew it down before it was finished.

PAYNESVILLE CHURCHES.

The Congregational church was organized in July 27th, 1866. Its meetings were held in a small chapel until 1872, when their present house of worship was built. Their first officers elected in 1866 were: John Lester, deacon; D. S. Twichell, clerk. The first trustees were R. P. Gilbert, James Lester, H. P. Luce, John Lester and D. S. Twichell. S. B. Trembly was their first minister. He began preaching August 3d, 1767. Their present church was built in 1872. Prior to that they held their meetings in a small chapel.

METHODIST EPISCOPAL CHURCH.

The Methodist Episcopal church was organized in 1859 with a membership of thirteen. Their first minister, Rev. W. N. Darnell, began preaching in 1859, and remained until 1862, when he enlisted in the army. Up to that time their meetings had been held in private houses. In the spring of 1862 a small house of worship was erected, but in September it was burned by the Indians in their attack on the fort.

George W. Bennett preached occasionally in 1862. But on account of the outbreak there was no record kept, and there seems to be no written record of this church prior to 1864 that can be found only in the memory of its early members.

EVANGELICAL ASSOCIATION.

Zion's church of the Evangelical Association situated on the east line of the town was organized August 15th, 1864, with a membership of about fifteen, but now in 1895 it has eighty-eight. Its first officers, Christ. Rien, Sen.; Fred Schroeder, and John Schoenleben, Sen. Their first minister was C. Lahr, followed C. Brill and F. Emde. The Evangelical Association situated in the village of Paynesville was organized in 1893, and their church building was erected the same year. Its trustees are John Baitenger, C. A. Zabel, F. Frank.

EPISCOPAL CHURCH.

New Paynesville Parish of St. Stephen, so-called because the first service was held on St. Stephen's day, 1888, was organized in July, 1888. Its officers are: A. Haines, Senior Warden; A. T. Watson, J. W. Vestrymen: Messrs. W. Haines, J. C. Harris, J. H. Boylan, Geo. R. Stephens, Dr. Griffin, S. R. Copeland, J. Fair and H. Baugh. W Haines, treasurer; G. R. Stephens, clerk. Rev. Mr. Booth Willmar was the clergyman in charge of the parish and has remained so even since holding services once in three months Mr. C. B. Fosbrook was lay reader in charge the first 2 years and Mr. A. Haines since.

The church was built in '88-'89 at a cost of $3000 of which there still remains a debt of about $600. There were five communicants when organized. A. Haines, Mrs. Baugh, Mrs C. J. LaGrave, Mrs. A. T. Watson, and A. T. Watson. We have now between 40 and 50 communicants.

ORGANIZATION OF THE TOWN.

In 1858 the town of Verndale had been organized, including what are now known as the towns of Lake Henry, Crow River, Crow Lake, North Fork, Lake George, Paynesville and half of St. Martin. Paynesville was organized as a separate town in 1867. The following is taken from the town records of its first meeting: "First town meeting was held September 23d, 1867, at the house of John Phipps. E. H. Bates was chosen moderator; I. L. Wait, H. H. Randolf and John Baitenger, judges; J. B. Pease, clerk. The officers for the remainder of this year were chosen by ballot. L. Elliot, chairman; John Baitenger, R. P. Gilbert, supervisors; J. B. Pease and H. H. Randolf, justices, Alfred Harris, constable; J. B. Pease, town clerk; R. P. Gilbert, treasurer; A Chisholm, overseer of highways district No 1; Alfred Harris, overseer of highways district No. 2; A. Wartonburg, overseer of highways district No. 3 No money was voted raised. 29 votes cast I hereby certify the above minutes to be correct.

"J B Pease, Clerk "

For ten long years the early settlers of this exposed frontier town had bravely and uncomplainingly battled with the hardships and privations of pioneer life. Still they were always cheerful and maintained a high social and literary standing. Their literary societies held frequent meetings which were well attended and greatly enjoyed. Their social meetings were frequent and pleasant.

It then took four days to make the trip to St. Cloud with their ox teams Now the railroad train covers the distance in about an hour.

The town was now (in 1867) fast settling up. The village was growing and business was reviving. Comfortable homes were being built and prosperity and plenty reigned. The old settlers looked back upon their pioneer life as a sort of dream. With a kind adieu, the writer leaves them with their well earned happiness, hoping that some more capable writer will carry forward the history of this prosperous and enterprising town. Many thanks to those who have assisted in this work.

Last week the history of Paynesville, which has been running in the TIMES, was concluded. Below will be found a number of biographical sketches of early settlers of that town:

JAMES H. BOYLAN.

J. H. Boylan was one of the first settlers of Paynesville. He was born in Burns, New York, in 1834, and raised a farmer. He came to Minnesota in the spring of 1856. In October of that year he arrived in Paynesville and took a claim and began its improvement. In 1859 Mr. Boylan married Miss Canrissia Richardson, at Cold Spring. In 1861 they went to New York and remained there until 1867 and then they returned to the farm which Mr. Boylan has operated ever since. For the last eleven years he has resided in the village of Paynesville. He has been a member of the town board since 1869, and a member of the school board in district No. 43 for twenty-one years and was postmaster under Buchanan and Cleveland 6 years and is now president of the Boylan and Brackett bank of New Paynesville.

W. P. BENNETT.

W. P. Bennett was born in Burns, New York, May 7th, 1825, and grew up a farmer. He graduated at a high school in Livingston county, N. Y. Mr. Bennett and Miss Mary J. Trembly were married in 1853, and in the fall of 1856 they came o Anoka, and in July of 1857 they came to Paynesville and located a claim and began improving it. They lived in the village until the fall of 1860 when they move l on to their claim. He was justice of the peace for many years and has held other town offices. He was assessor when

several townships were joined in one town called Verdale.

JOHN BAITENGER.

John Baitenger has been so intimately connected with all of the town affairs that the history of Paynesville would be incomplete without mentioning him. He was born in Wertenberg, Germany, in 1833. His principal occupation in that country was the raising of grapes and making wine. In 1853 he came to New York and worked one year on a farm, and then learned the cooper's trade. The next year Mr. Baitenger and Miss Fredricka Yeager were married. In 1856 they came St. Cloud and built a house and remained one year when they settled in Eden Lake on section six, near the line of Paynesville, and in 1866 moved over into that town and took a claim of 160 acres. Mr. Baitenger was chairman of the supervisors of the town of Verdale, and has been a member of the town board of Paynesville for many years. He was postmaster from 1870 to 1887 of the postoffice of Zion. He was intimately identified with the Evangelical Association, and was their first Sunday school superintendent. His beautiful farm with its fine buildings shows careful and intelligent management. He has lived in the village of Paynesville for a number of years.

HUGH BLAKELY.

Hugh Blakely was born in Ontario, Canada, in 1838. He came to Hastings, Minnesota, in 1856, where he remained two years, then coming to Paynesville and taking a claim. Up to this time his principal occupation had been carpentering. He improved his farm and erected buildings on it and remained on it until 1873, when he bought his present farm of two hundred and forty acres and moved upon it and improved it and has remained upon and operated it ever since. Mr. Blakely has been a prominent person in town and county affairs, having held the office of justice of the peace seventeen years, and county commissioner of Monongalie county three years, as well as being on the school board for many years.

JOHN BLAKELY.

John Blakely was born in the north of Ireland in 1821. He accompanied his family to upper Canada in 1825, where he was engaged in farming, surveying and lumbering until 1851, when he came to Minnesota and stopped at Hastings, until 1852. His wife was the first white woman that crossed the Mississippi from Point Douglas to Hastings. In 1858 he moved to Roseville, Kandiyohi county, and located on land half a mile west of his present farm, on which he moved in 1862. Mr. Blakely married Miss Jane Mooney in 1842. She died in 1889. He has been a member of the school board twelve years.

DANIEL CHISHOLM.

Daniel Chisholm, a native of Nova Scotia, was born in 1833. He emigrated with his family to Beaver Dam, Wisconsin, in 1847, where he remained until 1859, when he came to Paynesville and bought a farm and operated and improved it, but lived in the village. In 1862 they were driven away by the Indians, and during these stirring times he moved to St. Cloud and remained about a year, after which he returned to his farm. Mr. Chisholm and Miss Marietta Reed were married in 1855. He enlisted in the 1st Minnesota volunteer infantry in 1865 and served until the close of the war. He has been a farmer all his life. He has been a member of the town and school boards.

S. P. ROACH.

S. P. Roach was born in England April 14th, 1836. He emigrated with his family to the territory of Wisconsin in 1844, and remained there until 1857, when he came to Minnesota and settled in Houston county. He was brought up on a farm. In 1860 he came to Paynesville and took a claim and began to build a house and improve his farm. In 1863 Mr. Roach and Miss Susan Hoover were married. He has operated this claim and other lands that he has bought, ever since. He has been chairman of the Board of Supervisors

for some time and a member of the school board for twenty-two years. He entered the army in 1864, and served about one year. He has taken great interest in town and state affairs as well as in school matters.

JOHN PHIPPS.

Among the prominent early settlers of Paynesville we find John Phipps, who was born in Lawrence county, Indiana, in 1825 and was raised on a farm. In 1853 he went to Illinois and bought some wild land and improved it. In 1859 he came to Minnesota and located at Silver Creek, and remained there one year. He then came to Paynesville in February, 1860, and bought the farm that he still owns and operates. For the last twenty years Mr. Phipps has been in connection with his son, engaged in the general merchandise and furniture business. In March, 1865, he enlisted in Company A, 1st Minnesota Regiment, and served until the close of the war. He was assessor of the town of Verndale and also a member of the town board of supervisors.

ALFRED HARRIS.

Alfred Harris was born in New York in 1840. In 1860 he accompanied his parents to Green Lake, Kandiyohi county. In 1861 he came to Paynesville and took a claim and improved and operated it until 1883, when he sold his farm and moved to Lincoln county and bought a farm and operated it three years. Then he returned and located in the village of Paynesville, where he has since resided. In August, 1862, he enlisted in the army and served until the close of the war. He was elected constable when the town was organized in 1867, and has held the office twenty-four years.

ALEXANDER CHISHOLM.

Alexander Chisholm was born in Nova Scotia in 1847, and when two years old accompanied his parents to Wisconsin. His parents were farmers. In the fall of 1862 he came to Paynesville and worked for the Burbank Stage Company for four years. He then bought 280 acres of land, on which the Great Northern station now stands, and has operated it ever since. Mr. Chisholm has been prominent in political matters and has taken a deep interest in town and state affairs. He represented his district in the legislature in 1873 and also in 1895. He has been one of the town board for many years.

MICHAEL BECKLEY

Michael Beckly was born in Syracuse, N. Y., in 1831, and brought up on a farm. He came to Paynesville in 1862. He enlisted in the 7th regiment that same year and served three years, and then returned to his farm. In 1875 he built the lower flouring mill, called the Crow River mill, and has operated it in connection with his farm for the last twenty years. He is now in Kansas.

W. H. BLASDELL.

W. H. Blasdell was born in lower Canada in 1816 and lived on a farm. At the age of seventeen he accompanied his parents to Ohio. In 1842 he moved to Frankfort, Illinois, where he resided for twenty years, with the exception of four years, when he was sheriff of Will county and lived at Joliet. While in Illinois he was engaged in farming, lumbering and hotel business. In 1863 he came to Paynesville and took a claim and began farming and stock raising, as well as keeping a hotel. He was justice of the peace for many years and a member of the school board all the while that he lived there. Mr. Blasdell died April 24, 1887. His wife, who survives him, is still in good health and active, with a strong and vivid memory of their early pioneer life.

ROBERT OSTRANDER.

Egbert Ostrander, deceased, was a native of the State of New York, where he was born in 1815. He came to Illinois in 1837, locating at Kankakee, and thence to Paynesville in 1866, where he opened the Ostrander House on the 4th of July, 1873. He married Miss Delilah J. Sargent, of Indiana, in 1839. Their children are Henry M., Marietta, John Q., James E., Enoch M., Royal C., Hannah A., Elizabeth J. and William H. Mr. Ostrander died in September, 1878.

JOHN W. DARBY.

One of the prominent persons of Paynesville is John W. Darby, who was born in Cambridge, Washington county, New York, August 19, 1835. He remained there, attending school and working as a machinist, until 1853. He worked at his trade as a machinist in several states or attended school until 1863, when he enlisted and served until the close of the war. He was in General J. J. Bartlett's division, to which General Lee stacked arms at his surrender. After his return home his health was such that he could not work at his trade. He started west and stopped at Chicago until the spring of 1867, when he came to Paynesville, and in company with J. Moore, bought out J. L. Waite's store, and was appointed postmaster, retaining this office twenty-one years. He has held the office of justice of the peace, supervisor and town clerk. He married Miss Emma Elliott, of Canton, Pennsylvania, Jan. 15, 1870. They have one child, Bennett L.

A. E. BUGBIE

One of the later arrivals in the town was A. E. Bugbie, who was born in Holyoke, Mass., in 1849. When he was quite young he moved with his family to Belchertown, where he remained until fourteen years old. They then moved to Springfield, Mass. In 1868 he arrived in Paynesville. He had been a farmer. He taught school five years, then bought a farm and has operated it ever since. He has held some responsible offices nearly ever since his arrival in the town. He has served as town clerk twenty-two years; was assessor three years and three years a member of the School board.

.